SPORTS PSYCHING

Playing Your Best Game All of the Time

THOMAS TUTKO, Ph.D.
Co-founder, Institute of Athletic Motivation,
and Professor of Psychology, San Jose State University
AND UMBERTO TOSI

Jeremy P. Tarcher/Putnam
a member of
Penguin Putnam Inc.
New York

Jeremy P. Tarcher/Putnam
a member of
Penguin Putnam Inc.
375 Hudson Street
New York, NY 10014
www.penguinputnam.com

Library of Congress Catalog Card No.: 75-27975

Design by Marshall Licht/The Design element

Manufactured in the United States of America
40 39 38 37 36 35 34 33 32 31

SPORTS PSYCHING

Contents

SPORTS PSYCHING

GETTING A GRIP ON YOUR GAME:
The Need to Overcome the Pressures of Play

This book offers a coordinated system of techniques used by successful athletes for turning stress energy into better sports performance.

Lining up a putt you think, "If I make this one I'll have par—and maybe I can go on to break 90 for the first time in my life." And then suddenly a ton of pressure hits you, making you feel as if you were competing in the U.S. Open. And so you three-putt that hole, have trouble on the next, and wind up with a score pushing 100.

You look down a bowling alley and think, "As long as I don't get a split, I can win this one." And so, sure enough—you get a split.

You've just gotten in your last six straight serves, and your tennis opponent remarks, "Hey, man, you're on a streak!" The next thing you know, you double-fault—twice.

Millions of athletes face such stress situations all the time—and not just recreational players but also professional athletes, in both individual and team sports.

Yet though we know such stress affects us every time we go out to play we hear very little about how to deal with it. You can go to an instructor to correct your swing, but who's going to show you how to build confidence, ease up on anxieties, or shut out distractions that undermine your game? There are many books to help you improve the physical side of your game—books that show you how to grip the bat, club, racquet, ball, or pole—but what is there that shows you how to get a better grip on the self-consciousness, fears, angers, frustrations, and other emotional hassles that ruin sports performance?

That's what this book is all about. *Sports Psyching* gives you the tools to overcome these nonphysical problems and realize your athletic potential. It teaches you how to recognize the emotional and motivational factors in athletics and put them under your control. Our goal can be summarized in a single vision: *Recall the best day you ever had at your sport*—the day you were "hot," the day your moves were flawless, when you seemed able to put the ball where you really wanted to, to make your equipment respond to your every whim. That's the day we're going to try to give back to you—again and again.

As a psychologist, I have long been interested in the mental and emotional aspects of sports, and over the past twelve years I have worked directly with thousands of athletes and coaches trying to understand and overcome the intangibles that destroy athletic fulfillment. I have had the opportunity to work with, observe, and advise a number of professional teams. In basketball they include the former San Francisco Warriors and the San Diego Rockets. In baseball they include the Oakland A's and the Pittsburgh Pirates. The pro football teams I've spent time with make up a pretty fair list: the Steelers, the Cowboys, the Rams, the Dolphins, the '49ers, the Lions, the Saints, and the Broncos.

In addition, I have advised many college and high school teams, and have more recently become connected with Little League and Bobby Sox League teams, trying to help athletes and coaches on all levels find ways to achieve their best.

When I began this work, in the early 1960s, "psychology" was a scare word in sports. The general impression among managers and players was that a psychologist was someone who helped people who were disturbed or maladjusted. Coaches were afraid that if the public found out I was working with their players, people would think the team was crazy. Consequently, a great deal of my work was done under extremely confidential (and sometimes comical) conditions. One team director, for instance, insisted we have our meetings late at night in a remote motel so that the newspapers would not get wind of it. Ironically, his team's psychological problems—lack of morale, player disputes, and the like—had been public knowledge for years. Another athletic director, fearing the title "psychologist" would imply I was there to treat mental illness, referred to me (when he had to) as the "team behavioral scientist."

Today the situation has changed. The psychologist in sports is no longer viewed as someone probing the inner depths for signs of mental instability. Rather he is seen as a *teacher*, one who can share his knowledge of the emotional and learning problems that face every athlete and turn that understanding to constructive ends. And the field of sports psychology, once thought to be on a level with voodoo, has come into its own. Indeed, although it is relatively new in the United States, the Soviets have successfully used it in sports competition, one example being the Ukrainian bicyclist who won the 1972 Olympic gold medal partly as a result of his training in various psychotherapeutic methods. And the discipline has been developed to a high degree in Japan, Czechoslovakia, and East Germany, as well as in

Italy, which recently hosted the first International Congress on the Psychology of Sports.

This book takes a three-step route I have seen help many athletes overcome the psychological impediments to good performance and full enjoyment. The steps form a natural sequence that can be used no matter what your current proficiency and what your sport, whether individual or team.

The first step is to alert you fully to the psychological dimensions of all games. These concepts apply to anyone participating in athletics, and it is important to grasp them clearly. They have been greatly neglected in the literature and instructions relating to sports, yet they underlie everything we do on the playing field and are the main reasons we take part in athletics in the first place.

The second step is to make you aware of how these psychological elements affect your game. Many of my observations in this area come from years of working with my colleague at San Jose State University, Dr. Bruce Ogilvie, at our Institute of Athletic Motivation, which we set up to help coaches work with athletes. Out of this work have come several books intended to help players and coaches reach their maximum potential: *Problem Athletes and How to Handle Them* (1968), which I coauthored with Ogilvie; *The Psychology of Coaching* (1971) and *The Coach's Practical Guide to Athletic Motivation* (1972), both of which I wrote with coach Jack Richards; *Coaching Girls and Women: Psychological Perspectives* (1975), with Patsy Neal; and *Winning Is Everything and Other American Myths* (1976), with Bill Bruns. To further promote understanding among athletes. Mr. Lee Lyon, Dr. Ogilvie, and I devised a test called the Athletic Motivation Inventory (AMI), which was developed and revised over a five-year period and has been given to more than 75,000 athletes—professional, college, junior college, and high school— participating in a wide variety of sports. (More detailed information on it may be found in the appendix.) Because the AMI is a tool for the special needs of coaches and players in competitive sports, I have devised another kind of psychological test, an inventory on emotion, for this book. It is called the Sports Emotional-Reaction Profile (SERP), and it is designed for the individual recreational athlete. This SERP is designed to help you become more aware of psychological problem areas that can interfere with your game.

Once you have become aware of any problems, we will proceed to the third step—giving you specific techniques to deal with them. The techniques are based on my observations of professional and top college players, who obviously must learn to handle the psychological side of their game (or else settle for short, if perhaps flamboyant, careers). When I was first working with such players, I thought their psychological problems were really as special as their skills— more intricate and deeper than those most recreational athletes have. Later, however, I began to realize that amateurs shared the same difficulties—that although there is a world of difference in skills between the 145 amateur bowler and the 225 professional, there is less difference on an emotional level. It followed that the same psychological solutions many pros use could also benefit amateurs.

All successful players have found a system for dealing with the psychological stresses of their game. Before a game, you see some kid around, some pray, some become hyperactive, and some become almost comatose (even falling asleep, to deny any cause for anxiety). And almost all players have certain physical mannerisms that help them deal with stress. They may not know *why* they pull the left ear or stretch or chew gum, just that it seems to make them feel better. And because they adopted such methods by unconscious trial and error, they don't necessarily have control over when to employ them. However, most success-ful players have discovered *repeatable, self-controlled* ways of converting stress energies into productive drives.

These techniques are neither mysterious nor complicated. Nor are they unique to a special kind of person; any player can use them. The techniques are not only effective against choking, jitters, self-consciousness, anxiety, anger, lack of confidence, and all the other emotional problems that ruin sports performances, they also contribute to an injury-free game, for it is the emotional hassles we encounter in sports that often lead to strain and injury. Finally, they help make athletics the rewarding, joyful experience it is supposed to be.

You may wonder if this well-played, injury-free, joyful game is really possible for you. You may even be resigned to missing "the big one" and feel it hopeless to try to change. (After all, some habits seem so ingrained as to be inaccessible to solution.) I guarantee this is not so. Change is possible. This is not only the experience of thousands of athletes, but my own personal experience as well.

I used to play golf a lot. Not very well, but passionately. I wanted to be a top-flight golfer. I wanted to win, but somehow, in spite of lessons and trying very hard, my game didn't get much better. Indeed, the harder I tried the worse it seemed to get. When I approached the ball, my posture looked like that of an 85-year-old arthritic: completely rigid. And not only physically, but mentally. Golf was no longer fun, and the only enjoyable part came after the game was over and we had a few beers in the clubhouse. Though I was not aware of it, my anxiety was apparently causing me to try to hit the ball as hard as possible, and the resultant "muscling" caused me to shank shots—which caused more anxiety, and so on. Because of this cycle of frustration and defeat, I eventually gave up playing.

Later, as I became more involved in sports psychology, I realized what had happened to me and went back to the game. Using techniques like those presented here, I learned to relax and get fully into the action, leaving behind my anxieties. My attitude toward the game changed. My swing changed. My score changed, too—not dramatically from that which I used to rack up on my best days, but I found I was having my best day more often. Now I'm playing better and, boy, am I enjoying it more!

Perhaps you're still thinking, "Ah, I don't need this psychological stuff to whip my game into shape. It's just a matter of trying harder." I assure you "trying harder" won't do it. Not trying harder on the field, anyway. The area where more effort will work is in the psychological area. Of course, you might not want to discover or think about your psychological liabilities. Most people don't. However, I'm not interested in criticism, only in self-examination. The object is not to sit in judgment of yourself or chastise yourself for real and imagined failings. It is to take a realistic look at just how you react emotionally in athletics and with that realistic assessment work to change your game for the better.

There is nothing mystical about the emotional side of sports. Such matters can be defined and dealt with in deliberate, rational ways. I am not a psychotherapist dealing with deep-set emotional problems, or a Zen master trying to bring his students to a higher level of consciousness. The frame of reference is the main experience of all people who play at sports.

Obviously, you can't control the weather or field conditions. You can't change the laws of nature applying to the trajectory of the ball. You can't change luck and you can't change the other players (much). But you *can* be in control of yourself and your emotions—and thereby play your own game.

2

UP FROM EXERCISE:
Our Physical Overeducation

From the standpoint of the techniques of physical development in sports, we can truly say we live in a Golden Age.

We are overeducated on the physical side of sports. We act as if a sport were little more than physical activity, a sophisticated set of calisthenics. We learn to play a game in terms of its physical moves—the stance, the grip on the bat or racquet, the swing of the club, where the elbow goes, when to snap the wrist, swivel the hips, bend the knee, and arch the back. Step, crouch, jump, kick, pivot, throw, hit, roll, dip—every required action is studied and practiced in the belief that if we master the motions we master the game. But, of course, it doesn't always happen that way.

There are teachers and coaches everywhere to impart the fundamentals to us. Television replays allow us to analyze the moves of professionals in slow motion. Tennis schools and golf driving ranges likewise are equipped with closed-circuit television for instant videotape analysis of our latest efforts. Clubs, gyms, and community centers hold sports clinics, with professional athletic heroes acting as consultants. Shelves groan with how-to books giving the inside stuff on every game's physical techniques. Daily newspaper columns dispense handy hints. Magazines analyze the latest advances in equipment and refinements of athletic skills, complete with graphs, diagrams, and computer-based analyses of velocity, inertia, and g-forces. The available data is overwhelming, and we diligently study as much of it as we can, searching for the secrets of athletic performance. But it doesn't always work.

Not only do we have access to a wealth of knowledge, we also have the most sophisticated tools to put that knowledge to work. Sporting goods stores offer a racquet for every hand, a special shoe for every sport (Adidas has 170 different kinds—and without any for bowlers), all designed, they tell us, with the aid of still more computers and other gee-whiz technology. The graphite shafts of golf clubs are of the same resilient substance as the wing tips of fighter planes. Bowling balls are milled with the precision of an orbital satellite. Technology is also liberally applied in developing practice gadgets. We can duel by the hour with machines that zing baseballs or tennis balls or even Ping-Pong balls at us. Homes, offices, and backyards are littered with self-training apparatus—hollow plastic bowling balls, putting practice gizmos, rubber rebounders. Most are discarded after a while, their promise unfulfilled.

We approach sports as a physical challenge, to be met with the proper application of muscle, know-how, and noble effort. If hours spent practicing the game itself don't seem enough, we may believe some body conditioning is in order. Once again, the techniques and the hardware are abundant. We can jog or do isotonics at the office. We can join a gym and use its arsenal of muscle-building equipment. Special exercises go with each sport: skiers do their leg presses; tennis players swing weighted racquets and do double knee jumps; golfers swing kitchen brooms to build arm and shoulder muscles. All this exercise may produce healthier duffers, but it may not improve the scores a whit.

Likewise with nutrition: who can quarrel with eating what's good for you? Even if there's no scientifically established link between special diets and souped-up athletic performance. Thus, many athletes wash down megavitamins with organic carrot-watercress cocktails spiked with soya powder and brewer's yeast. Some professional teams even have "nutritional advisors." One, for example, urged NFL players to eat high-protein meals in the days following a Sunday game, in order to help rebuild injured tissue; later in the week starchier foods were advised, to build energy reserves for the upcoming week's contest. Eating right may keep you fit, but how much does it help your golf handicap?

Looking at the physical side of sports, then, we can truly say we are living in a Golden Age, and we can follow its royal roads as far as our bodies and our ambitions dictate. No area of physical education, it seems, is undeveloped. But though we are physically overeducated, we are emotionally undereducated.

OUR EMOTIONAL UNDEREDUCATION

The psychological factors are the most important yet the most neglected in our approach to sports.

Most great athletes acknowledge state of mind as the key to success in sports. "Once you are physically capable of winning a gold medal," Olympic hurdler Patti Johnson says, "the rest is 90 percent mental." Baseball, Maury Wills says, is "all mental." The psychological aspect, Rams' linebacker Charlie Cowan says, is "the most important thing in football or any other sport." We could gather a thousand quotes from a thousand athletes to express this thought.

Yet the psychological side of athletics is uncharted territory for most players. They wander in it with maps about as reliable as those of 15th-century navigators. Most of what we hear about the psychological dynamics of sports is contradictory, vague, or misleading. It consists of exhortations, heard from Little League onwards, to "have a winning attitude," to "fire yourself up" while "staying cool," to "hang in there"—all variations on "thinking positive."

Most of this doesn't help. If anything, it probably hurts. Amazingly, very few of us really have any clear notion of just what a "winning attitude" is—how it feels and how to bring it on. Every time you lose, you may think, "I guess I didn't have a winning attitude" and feel guilty for not thinking positively.

Actually, the positive thinking we are supposed to do might well be labeled wishful thinking, and usually it creates more fears than it dissipates. For one thing, it is too goal-oriented to help much in a sports situation. You are supposed to say to yourself, "I *will* win," or "I *will* score a point." But it doesn't help you concentrate on how to attain those goals, on the moves you need to make a certain play succeed, and so on. As Timothy Gallwey, former Harvard tennis team captain and author of the best-selling book, *The Inner Game of Tennis*, points out, all you may succeed in doing when you concentrate on such slogans is to remind yourself that the reverse might come true. When you say, "I must win," you emphasize as well the possibility that the opposite can happen. Thus, positive thinking becomes a form of negative thinking.

Prevailing ideas also have it that it is your duty to "psych yourself up," to work yourself into a lather for every game. This idea, too, is destructive. It gives you no way to differentiate between being "up"—i.e., enthusiastic and self-confident—and being desperate to win at all costs.

On the whole, the psyching-up idea is more part of the problem than a solution. Dr. Robert M. Neideffer of the University of Buffalo, a clinical psychologist who has worked extensively with athletes, says: "All this rah-rah stuff is generally bad. Nine times out of ten, the arousal technique generates pressure and performance suffers." Locker-room pep talks and similar exhortations, he finds, only add to anxieties about winning. Players who do well do so *despite* this goading rather than because of it.

This isn't to say that a charismatic or dynamic coach can't inspire a team to an extraordinary effort; it's just that, applied to most of us, the method usually has a reverse effect. Most recreational players don't need to be pushed to try harder. They are already trying too hard as is. Thus, there is little in the traditional approach to sports to help us to understand and deal effectively with the psychological part of the experience. We are left to improvise and muddle through.

GREAT EXPECTATIONS DENIED

Why athletes tend to get just so good and no better.

In spite of its failings, the conventional, physical approach to athletics works to a degree. Some of us play well much of the time. A few get to be very good indeed. Most of us get to be not so hot. The usual result of taking up a sport is for the player to reach the point of being able to participate, but frequently with a sense of dissatisfaction, a feeling that his performance just isn't what it should be.

And that's usually right, for the truth is that just about

everyone could play a better game. Most of us reach pla-
teaus in our playing ability, where improvement levels off
and performance may even dip. The development of our
game gets stuck. (Most of us would ask, "Why couldn't it
have gotten stuck on a little higher plane?") Redoubled
practice may bring diminishing returns. Additional lessons
may produce only a temporary upgrading in our game, and
that fact makes the plateau all the more frustrating. We
know we can do better—dammit, we *have* done better—
but . . .

This is the point where many players, especially weekend
athletes, throw up their hands—and frequently throw down
their clubs and racquets. They become depressed ("God, I'm
hopeless!") or angry at themselves ("Dummy, hit it right!").
They may alibi, swear at their equipment (or the court or
the wind), or mutter envious curses at co-players. After a
while, many athletes begin to figure this is it. "The harder I
try, the worse I get," they say. "I can't do any better." And
they resign themselves to having a body that only occasionally will do what they know it can do.

Most people give up too soon. They are unprepared for
the plateau and the emotional problems they meet there.
When you are a beginner, progress is usually more dramatic
and thus more rewarding. After overcoming initial feelings
of clumsiness, you start making shots—*voilá,* the tennis ball
sails over the net and, miracle of miracles, into the other
court! The golf ball flies straight and long and true; the
bowling ball no longer skids into the gutter; the arrow finds
its target. Success becomes frequent enough to enable you
to participate in regular games. These early strides raise
expectations. If one shot goes well, then another, then
another—you figure, why not all the rest? The improvement
from the day you first pick up your racquet to the day of
your first real game also seems spectacular, so you look in

vain for further *spectacular* improvement, expecting soon to be serving aces at 100 m.p.h.

But an advance from a shaky game to a strong one does not involve as rapid a metamorphosis as happened at first. Now improvements are more subtle. It isn't just a matter of learning new shots, but of consistently using the ones you've already learned—and using them under the pressures of competitive play.

Usually what is holding you back isn't a lack of physical ability. No doubt you have sometimes thought to yourself, "I know how to make this move correctly. I am physically *able* to make this move correctly. I *want* to make this move correctly. So why the hell do I keep blowing it?"

You won't find the answer in the physically oriented instruction manuals. You'll find it in yourself.

3

MORE THAN MUSCLES:
The Emotional Content of Sports

Why do we all get so excited over sports?

Probably no area of life produces more excitement but less profit personally than spectator sports do for their fans, yet it is obvious they offer meaningful rewards to millions of people. You can hardly call such games relaxing, given the tension they provoke in most viewers, but they certainly are distracting. They bring uncertainty and excitement into routine lives. They offer vicarious satisfaction by identification. They give one the opportunity to see and be inspired by what an individual or a team can accomplish with talent and effort.

But after the game is over, does it really matter whether the Packers or the Warriors or the Giants or the Blackhawks won or lost? Besides the owners, the players, the gamblers, and the bookies, how many of us gain in any significant way from the outcome of any athletic contest we watch? Yet throughout the world, spectator sports are one of mankind's great obsessions.

Millions of people spend a large part of their available

money and available time watching teams perform at stadiums and on television; 73 million people—78 percent of the TV audience—watched the 1976 Superbowl on TV, for example. Many will also enjoy replays of the game on the evening news, go on to read about it in the paper next morning, discuss it the next day with people at work, and even catch it again in *Sports Illustrated* the following week. Friends get into fights over sports. Couples get divorced over sports. Rioters tear stadiums apart—and occasionally referees—over the outcome of a game. And all this is just over watching *other* people play.

When we participate ourselves, these passions are felt more personally, but in the great scheme of things could be considered just as irrational. While playing what are supposed to be relaxing Sunday games, we behave in ways that would be regarded as signs of being mentally unbalanced if we did them off the field. We talk to ourselves. We curse inanimate objects. We throw things, become aggressive toward friends, and sometimes we even cheat (because the appearance of winning becomes more important than our self-respect). What pressures push us to these actions?

Playing in a game is obviously not just a physical experience; it is a total personal experience. You don't leave your personality, habits, and attitudes behind when you walk onto the field. What you do there is recognized as "physical activity," but the movement of every muscle involves you emotionally. And it is the emotional charge—the feeling side of sport—that makes it so fascinating, exciting, and frustrating.

This emotional charge comes from many directions. First, there are the *intrinsic* pressures to overcome the physical challenge which is part of every game. Second, there are the *cultural* pressures from our society, which sets great store on superior athletic performance. Third, there are the *personal* pressures, which derive from your own athletic experience and the ways you have learned to react to it. Recognizing these elements, as much as understanding your grip or your stance, will help you to know why you so often don't do what you know you can do when you're out on the field.

THE INTRINSIC PRESSURES OF SPORTS

The challenge of uncertainty, competition, and luck.

Every sport provides the athlete with a specific set of challenges: making a basket, getting the ball over the net, hitting the pins, and so on. Indeed, the tasks in each game are meaningless except in terms of testing your ability to do them. The *uncertainty* of the outcome of that test is what makes a game interesting.

But uncertainty also automatically makes the game anxiety-producing. One always wonders, "Will I make it?", and no player, no matter how good, is immune from this concern. Wimbledon champion Arthur Ashe, for example, says he used to have seizures of fear before almost every game. He would think, "What if I go through the whole match and can't return a single serve?"—not can't win or can't return the opponent's best serve, but can't return a *single* serve. This is an unlikely prospect for a beginner, no less a tournament player, but it can seem not all that unlikely to an anxiety-fed imagination during play.

Another intrinsic source of pressure is the *competition*. Most games are social in nature and involve not only overcoming a physical challenge but doing so better than someone else. In our society, which is already heavily oriented toward competition, even play becomes a test of superiority.

Where you are not matching your abilities directly against

an opponent, it is expected that you will play against yourself or measure your performance against the standards of the game. So you try to top your best score, beat par, go for some record. You may spend five dollars in a pinball machine to win one free game, try to jog a mile farther than you ever have, risk a hernia with a press twenty-five pounds over what you've managed before. With or without an opponent, there is competition, because games involve scores and measurements to test, challenge, and lure you on—and to constantly remind you of the chances for failure, frustration, and defeat.

The challenges of the various tasks required in sports and of having to accomplish these tasks against competition or a fixed standard are automatic setups for psychological distress, for they lead us to grading our performance. Sometimes we may judge ourselves as very good because we reached a certain goal or defeated an opponent. Or we may feel dissatisfied even upon having reached the goal because we didn't reach it before others. Or having outdone others, we may still feel that we should have done better. A judgment of how well we did emerges from every sports contest. And because there is almost always someone who does it better or faster (possibly in front of our eyes), many of the judgments we make about ourselves tend to be essentially negative.

A third important element intrinsic to every sport is _luck_. No matter how well you play, there's no accounting for wind, weather, field conditions, odd bounces, or even an opponent who suddenly may be playing the best game of his life (would that it were you!). It is very easy to construct a chain of events in which one different bounce of the ball could change the entire outcome of any close contest. A punt returned for a touchdown could have bounced to the left and out of bounds instead of the right

and into the runner's hands. A tie-breaking hit could have
gone just an inch to the foul side of the chalk line. The
professionals know this well. Just before one game of the.
Boston-Cincinnati 1975 World Series, Redlegs manager
Sparky Anderson said he believed the outcome between the
two evenly matched teams would be decided by luck. And
he was right. One game in this 4 to 3 series was decided by
an umpire's disputed ruling. Who can say under such hair-
splitting circumstances that the better team won?

Like the other intrinsic factors, this unpredictable element is one of the things that makes athletics interesting.
But it, too, is unnerving. Although the law of averages dic-
tates that in the long run the good breaks and bad breaks
will be even, from a psychological viewpoint the bad always
outweighs the good. Unlucky breaks are a source of emotional challenge because they can make you angry or discouraged and present you with the problem of absorbing
them without losing your emotional equilibrium. Moreover,
you are apt to remember and be affected by the bad breaks
long after the good ones are forgotten.

Obviously, the multiple pressures inherent in any game
are hard enough to cope with psychologically without there
being any others. But society, too, lays a heavy emotional
load on our shoulders.

THE SOCIAL PRESSURES
OF SPORTS

The fate worse than death.

Most of us uncritically and unconsciously accept the
professional model of sports as being essentially appropriate

for us. In this model, several things are held up as desirable: winning is worshipped, the athlete is considered the super-hero, the greatest goal is record breaking, and the ability to absorb physical punishment is proof of character, as is the ability to stay cool under stress. The ultimate statement of the professional model is the famous assertion attributed to the late Green Bay Packer coach Vince Lombardi: "Winning isn't everything—it's the only thing." This ardor for victory is expressed in collegiate sports, too. When Bill Musselman was University of Minnesota basketball coach, a sign was posted over the entrance to the team shower that read: DEFEAT IS WORSE THAN DEATH, BECAUSE YOU HAVE TO LIVE WITH DEFEAT. And even some great winning coaches have found defeat unspeakably terrible—after Ohio State lost to UCLA in the 1976 Rose Bowl, coach Woody Hayes snubbed re-porters not only after the game but for a full month afterward.

A classic example of the message we receive from the mass media about the significance of victory was when one of the television networks aired a short film recapping the Pittsburgh Steelers' 1975 Super Bowl victory. The back-ground audio was not commentary on the game but a recording of Robert Goulet singing "The Impossible Dream" from *Man of La Mancha.* The lyrics about fighting the unbeatable foe and reaching the unreachable stars might well be appropriate background for man's landing on the moon, but to use them to exalt a bunch of guys moving a ball around seems ludicrous. If you are a professional player, I can see why you might be willing to fight the unbeatable foe since you might reach the unreachable sal-ary. But what about the Little Leaguer or high school athlete or the recreational player who is in sports sup-posedly for personal satisfaction? He, too, buys the "im-possible dream" fantasy for a cause—the glory of winning.

The emotional roots of athletics are deep. A great deal of the jargon and many of the attitudes about sports have been carried over from the days when games were rites of passage in primitive societies. Games have always been training for serious competition. The British, for example, were said to have won their wars on the playing fields of Eton, where the officer class learned as children the importance of sacrificing to win. Games are a sublimation of combat between individuals or between cities, regions, or countries. In the Middle Ages, some games were little more than ceremonial warfare, as when knights jousted—sometimes to the death—or when the entire male populations of opposing towns played a form of soccer in a no-holds-barred contest to move the ball into the adversary's territory. In modern games, warfare metaphors still abound: competing sides alternately play "offense" or "defense," this team "destroyed" that one, so-and-so has a "killer instinct," a long pass is a "bomb," overtime play is "sudden death" (note the equating of death-as-losing, and the emphasis on sudden losing as opposed to sudden winning).

As great warriors have always been great heroes, the warriors of our time, the professional athletes, now often receive the social benefits of generals. The process starts in the schoolyard. The kids who are best in sports are generally the most popular, and those who perform poorly are often scorned. Repeatedly being the last one picked when kids choose up sides can leave lifelong emotional scars; there is always the feeling when you play you are somehow being tested, being judged as a person as well as a player. Although in later life we deemphasize this, even as adults we find that being a superior player in a leisure sport rates social points with whatever group we're in. (You may have no idea how good your doctor is at tennis, but in subtle ways his game may affect his position on the hospital staff.)

Few things make heroes (or rich men) as quickly as the breaking of records—which we are constantly reminded by the media are "made to be broken." Much of society's focus in athletics, therefore, is on the superhuman feat. We look for the great play, the great game, the great season, paying scant attention to the fact that championships are built on percentages, little moments. Jack Nicklaus's scoring average, for example, as top man on the Professional Golf Association tour in 1975, was 69.88; Jim Simmons, who ranked fiftieth, averaged 71.89—less than two strokes difference. You might not openly espouse this *Guinness Book of World Records* philosophy when you go out for a weekend game. You may, in fact, deny you feel that way. But if you are playing ball in the 1970s, it's hard to escape from carrying these attitudes around with you.

Records also are frequently the product of playing through pain. In track and field events, and in swimming particularly, an athlete's high pain threshold may be as significant as his basic ability. And if the professionals can play with sprains and strains and even broken bones, as we are constantly and admiringly told they do, why can't we? This never-say-die attitude, rather than enriching life and health, can even lead to a termination of it. Quite a few middle-aged tennis players have felt compelled to complete five sets because "that's the way the game is played" (by twenty-five-year-olds, they forget) and afterwards collapsed from a heart attack. No doubt you yourself sometimes have pushed beyond what your physical condition permits, with resulting sprains, torn ligaments, and the like.

Professional athletics is pure business, and at times its effects are dehumanizing on the players, as some of them have protested (such as Jim Bouton in *Ball Four* and Dave Megyessy in *Out of Our League*). But despite such calls for a reexamination of athletic goals, many amateur players still haven't realized that professional athletes are not appropriate models for anyone but other pros or pro-hopefuls. Physically, professionals are a specialized breed. Out of the millions of young Americans who play sports, only a handful make it into the professional ranks. Some professional football teams have field goal kickers who can kick a field goal 60 yards. Even a horse can't kick a ball that far.

The athlete as superhero has also fostered a false picture of how players should react to emotional stress. Having been involved with the stresses of a good many professional and college athletes, I can tell you the iron man myth is indeed a myth. Although sportscasters never fail to point out a winner overcame terrific pressure in a game, they generally ignore the times that athlete may have succumbed to such pressure. Moreover, professional players seldom talk about the times they were nervous. Thus, when the average player feels strongly pressured by the tensions of a particular match, he has no way of seeing that feeling as a part of the overall athletic experience. Rather, he views it with considerable self-criticism and guards it from the outside world.

Everyone seems to feel these self-doubts are his own dark secret. The really good players, we think, rarely have such problems. But they do, they really do. Some of them even admit it. In *The Education of a Tennis Player*, Rod Laver wrote words that should be memorized by every athlete: "Maybe it won't be much consolation, but you ought to know I've choked, still do sometimes, and most likely always will. And I haven't met anybody who hasn't." And Laver has met the very best.

But the pros, the special beings, have become models for millions of recreational athletes. They are held up to us in school gym classes, where each grade level operates as a proving ground for the next level and where less talented "undesirables" are weeded out and told, in so many words,

"Go sit on the bench." As a result, winning games, rather than playing, becomes the obsession. Professionalism, rather than participation, becomes the goal. And so you try to play tennis like Jimmy Connors or golf like Jack Nicklaus. And when you can't do it, you're unconsciously disappointed. Many Americans, therefore, have given up playing altogether, because of the impossible goals they unconsciously feel they must meet. And many of those left on the field are plagued by feelings of inferiority or of frustration at never being able to achieve such goals.

One class of athletes in particular suffers from this overemphasis, and that is women. A great many social pressures discourage women from participating in sports. They feel they are unable to engage in strenuous activity, that they are easily hurt, that they can't be feminine if they participate. Many men feel women are psychologically unable to cope with the stress of competition, and indeed in a society where many of the traits necessary for competition are not fostered in women—assertiveness, outspokenness, overcoming physical pain inflicted by others—it is not surprising so few have played in athletics to the limits of their potential. Fortunately, this situation seems to be changing, and the area of women in sports will probably be the one that undergoes the greatest expansion and flowering of any in the next decade.

Obviously, all these social pressures on amateur athletes have nothing to do with the intrinsic challenges of a particular game. They encourage us to make invidious comparisons of ourselves with players whose motivation and talents are on a level we can never reach. They narrow the value of the game to a simple test of performance, leaving out all of the other reasons—health, relaxation, sociability, or just the need to get out of the house—for which the recreational athlete plays.

THE PERSONAL PRESSURES
OF SPORTS

The biggest anxiety producer is you.

We are all social animals with the need to be liked and respected, to both fit in with others and yet to stand out sufficiently so that our individual worth is recognized. We are a mix of many emotions and drives, and many of them are in conflict with one another. On the game field, that conflict can turn to combat.

For most of us, the first source of personal pressure for athletic accomplishment is our parents. Most parents, often unconsciously, put tremendous pressure on their kids to perform. They reward the child only for superior performance, and if he doesn't prove to be pretty good pretty quickly, parental interest in that child's enjoyment of that sport is apt to disappear. Jim Piersall in his autobiography, *Fear Strikes Out*, tells a classic story of how parental pressure drove him to create unachievable expectations for himself. Even though he was an immensely talented and successful baseball player, it wasn't enough. He had to be the best, and his "failure" to reach that goal eventually led to a nervous breakdown. For most players, the results are not so disastrous, but still, parental pressures for athletic excellence are carried into adulthood by almost all of us, along with other aspects of how we feel about ourselves.

If you tend to feel insecure about whether people like you, this too can become a source of personal pressure in your game. You might fear ridicule when you are doing poorly or be afraid that others will dislike you if you beat them. A woman might feel that beating a man in a game would make him reject her as a future companion because of the humiliation of a loss to the "weaker" sex. Of all the pressures, one of the most difficult to face has to do with success, for we both want it and fear it. As each person becomes more capable, there is greater push to become more successful and more skilled. More often than not, there is the feeling that others expect it of you, and that no matter how well you do, short of a record-breaking performance, you're not doing well enough.

I once knew a successful salesman who shot a good game of golf, but unfortunately saw himself as his office's professional and thus felt he couldn't allow himself to lose. His golf matches soon became more than an opportunity for fun or relaxation; they were head-to-head confrontations to beat other people from his office and maintain his self-imposed status. He built in a level of challenge in his own mind that soon turned the other people in his office from golfing partners into golfing enemies and from business associates into rivals. Sadly, as he unnecessarily continued to increase this self-imposed pressure, his game deteriorated. He turned himself into a rival he could not beat.

Each sport, in addition, makes different demands on aspects of the athlete's personality and his ability to emotionally adapt himself to the requirements of the game. Even if you are well suited for a position physically, you also need to be suited for it psychologically. A football lineman requires a high level of aggressiveness but a different level of his control of it, depending upon whether he is playing offense or defense. Long-distance running requires self-discipline more than aggressiveness. Being an outfielder in baseball has different emotional requirements from being a center in basketball. And not only must each player tailor his emotions to the needs of his sport, he must do so at the right time. If you are trying to get in a second serve in tennis, but are boiling with rage at what you consider to be an inaccurate call by your opponent on your first serve, your chances of success are greatly diminished.

CAUGHT IN THE CROSS CURRENTS

Every athlete must deal with a combination of pressures.

The various pressures you feel in sports don't just act by themselves; they mix. They come at you from different directions and you are caught in the middle. One pressure makes you feel and act one way, while another says to act in the opposite way. For example, consider what may be happening in your head when you're lining up that short putt and you start thinking, "If I make this one, I'll be par and maybe break 90 for the first time in my life."

First, you came to the golf course with certain personal needs—to relax, of course, but also, let us say, to be sociable with a new business associate. But you're playing better than your usual game and are giving the other player a sound beating. While you feel good about winning, you also feel a bit embarrassed that he may think you lied about your handicap and worried about how he may take your really beating him.

Your personal needs, which already have an element of conflict in them, now run up against the societal pressures, for you are culturally conditioned to be a strong competitor and to go for the big one whenever you can. When you started the game, you expected to shoot no better than a 93. But now you realize you have a chance at an 89, your best score ever. Even if you miss, you could congratulate yourself on carding 90, but you want to go for the big one, too. Now it has become 89 or a washout. So, instead of feeling good about how well you have done, you now have cause for worry about how well you will have done after the putt.

Caught up in a welter of conflicting thoughts provoked

by contradictory personal and socially conditioned needs, is it any wonder that your palms get sweaty and your vision begins to blur just a little? If you are worried about losing friends, about having to prove yourself at the same time, about what the total score is, and what that means in the cosmic scheme of things, you are less likely to meet the intrinsic challenge of the putt. The imaginary, socially stimulated challenge of having to prove you could break 90 with the putt conflicts with the intrinsic challenge of what you have to do to make it, and perhaps with your own ambivalent feelings as well. Some fun.

Every athlete must deal with some combination of pressures. How you hit any shot, how you perform in any sport, is influenced by your own goals, personality, culturally conditioned beliefs, and personal beliefs about athletics, working together and against each other and interacting with the demands of your particular game. Let's see what the anxieties caused by these cross currents do to your athletic performance.

THE MIND
IS THE MATTER:
The "Fight or Flight" Syndrome

How psychological pressures are translated into physical performance problems.

Your emotions affect every cell in your body. Mind and body, mental and physical, are intertwined. The proof of this is the immense growth of the field that combines psychology and health, namely, psychosomatic medicine. There are physiological manifestations of what is on your mind and psychological reflections of what happens to you physically. Thus, you can become irritable because you have indigestion, or you can get indigestion because you are mentally irritated.

Whether the reasons for becoming emotional are real or imaginary, your reactions are similar. When you become anxious during a game—when you start to worry, "Will I make it? I've gotta get this hit or we're gonna lose"—your body starts to react almost as if the danger were not a lost game but a lost life. It goes into a state of preparedness for danger known as the "fight or flight" syndrome. We carry this behavior pattern with us from prehistoric times as a survival mechanism, and it works without our having to think about it. This automatic response was valuable if you were about to be trampled by a mastodon, but it has its disadvantages if you are trying to settle down and concentrate on the next play in a game.

THE MECHANICS OF "FIGHT OR FLIGHT"

We each have a biological alarm system that goes off automatically—whether we want it to or not.

Physically, "fight or flight" works this way. When you perceive a threat (real or imaginary), a signal goes to the hypothalamus, the walnut-sized part in the back of your head that acts as the central switchboard for brain and body functions. The hypothalamus releases a hormone that triggers the nearby pituitary gland. The pituitary in turn releases a strong hormone called ACTH, which sends a message through the rest of the body and stimulates your adrenal glands (just over your kidneys) into releasing still more hormones—adrenalin, cortisone, epinephrine, norepinephrine.

This potent cocktail tells various parts of your body to get ready for trouble. Your muscles tense, staying near the threshold of action. Your heartbeat and breathing speed up, and panting allows you to quickly get rid of the carbon dioxide in your system. The muscles of your bronchial tubes also tend to tighten, making your breathing not only faster but shallower—you literally tend to "choke."

Meanwhile, your whole digestive system shuts down, since you don't need to be digesting food if you are preparing for a fight or flight. Thus, your esophagus contracts and the gastric juices stop flowing. (This can make you feel nauseated and is a reason some athletes get sick to their stomachs before a big game. It was reported that even after ten years of dominating pro basketball, Bill Russell said he threw up before every game.

You also go into a kind of shock. Blood is diverted to the large muscles. Small blood vessels at your extremities and near the skin surface partially close down—a defense against bleeding to death should you be wounded. In addition, this gives you a clammy feeling, for the circulation is drawn away from your skin and so it gets cooler.

What I have described, in a simplified form, is the extreme reaction—real panic. Naturally, this doesn't happen to you every time you become intimidated in a sports situation, but if you become anxious, you do experience these symptoms to some degree. And since you are constantly under pressure of one sort or another in sports, your body is responding to whatever anxieties you feel as a result of these pressures.

Sometimes the response to "fight or flight" can be helpful. It can give you a quick burst of energy at the right moment, enabling you to go beyond your normal limitations and make a great effort. For example, basketball fans who were there will long remember Jerry West's spectacular winning shot, made from beyond midcourt, in the closing second of an NBA championship game between the Los Angeles Lakers and the New York Knicks. From a psychologist's point of view, it is not accidental that the shot was made by Jerry West, whose nickname, "Mr. Clutch," indicated his special ability to handle pressure and channel it into the game itself. Similar actions can happen off the field, too, as we know from reading about individuals who, in an extraordinary moment, have lifted a car off someone trapped beneath it. The energy of that moment of panic is channeled into one incredible effort.

However, it is far more common in athletics for anxieties and tensions to be disruptive—both physically, affecting your playing ability, and mentally, affecting your concentration and judgment.

THE PHYSICAL DISRUPTIONS

✳ *Emotional stress throws off your physical performance and literally makes you "choke."*

The "fight or flight" syndrome often comes at the wrong time and place in athletics. Instead of getting the shot of adrenalin just when you hit the ball, you may get it when you need to be coolly getting into position for the next play. Moreover, even if the adrenalin comes at the right time, and gives you a quick burst of energy, most of your body's reactions to this emotional jolt don't really do you much good. In fact, they usually disturb your physical performance. Here are six ways it happens:

(1) **"Choking," or shortness of breath.** The rapid shallow breathing that results from high anxiety can rob you of stamina for the long haul. In most games, you need to take deep, regular breaths to catch your wind between peak activity periods. You may notice top athletes take some deep breaths before each play period. They instinctively do this to counter the "fight or flight" tightening up of the chest.

(2) **Blurred vision.** Tension is sometimes manifested in the eye muscles, causing excessive watering of the eyes and impaired sight.

(3) **Death grip.** Excessive muscular tension tends to destroy the fluidity needed for successful performance. You can't

be loose. Your muscles become knotted and you cannot extend them fully to have the kind of limberness you need. Tennis players, for example, commonly get a death grip on their racquets when nervous. This tends to restrict their swing, inhibiting follow-through.

④ **Muscle fatigue.** Prolonged tension in your muscles can also tire you out faster. Your muscles stay tense instead of relaxing and becoming reinvigorated during breaks in the action.

⑤ **Disrupted coordination.** With anxiety, your muscles receive all kinds of contradictory messages, and your actions tend to reflect this, becoming more abrupt, never being fully committed to a movement but rather pulled this way and that. Part of you goes with the play, part of you goes with what's worrying you. For example, I know a championship swimmer who for a time was kept from reaching his potential because of an unconscious habit of looking over his shoulder while in a race—reflecting his fear that other swimmers might be gaining on him.

⑥ **Proneness to injury.** You are more likely to get hurt when you are tired and tense, especially if your coordination is disrupted and your movements only half-committed. When a muscle is tight, it shortens. This, in turn, shortens the connective tissue, called the fascia, which covers your muscles. A sudden jerk can tear the fascia, causing painful injury—lumbago when it happens in your lower back. Habitual tension over years' time also can cause the fascia to contract, thicken, and lose some of its elasticity, making it more vulnerable to tearing. Anxiety makes you a candidate for a wrenched knee or thrown-out back. And in the long run, as we all know, tension can produce such health problems as ulcers, high blood pressure, and heart disease.

THE MENTAL DISRUPTIONS

✳ *Emotional snowballing can affect your concentration and judgment.*

Every game makes mental demands. You have to concentrate on the action, for successful play requires full attention. You also must formulate and apply strategies and be able to adapt them quickly. In addition, you must remember and coordinate all the fundamental moves of your game. And you must remember and apply a set of rules and make judgments on them all the time. Finally, you must synthesize strategy, rules, assessments of your and other players' abilities, and of the weather and field conditions, into an on-going judgment of the situation, so as to make the best response.

Anxieties, however, make all these mental operations difficult. They distract you from the things you must keep in mind. One of the characteristics of the "fight or flight" syndrome is that it is cyclical. All those physiological manifestations—the shortness of breath, rapid heartbeat, nausea, claminess—are detected by the brain. The uncomfortable feelings in turn are psychologically alarming and produce even more mental distress, which then produces more physical response, and so on. You can prove this to yourself with a simple experiment. Try grimacing, making the most angry expression you can. If you hold this expression for a few moments, you probably will note that you actually start to *feel* angry, even though there was nothing for you to be sore about to start with. This is an elementary form of biofeedback. Your brain gets the message from your body that something is wrong and reacts to it.

This feedback response becomes a distraction in sports. Say you miss an easy shot in tennis. You become angry with yourself. The physical manifestations—tense muscles, faster breathing, etc.—begin setting in, making you irritable. And when your next shot comes up, your emotions rule your effort and you slam the ball—probably out, which gives you more to be angry about.

This cycle can work in as many ways as you can feel emotions. Anger, worry, embarrassment, fear, frustration, discouragement, guilt—all can have a similar disruptive effect on your thinking, concentration, and alertness during a game. Unrecognized, unchecked emotional problems in sports have an emotional snowballing effect. Anxiety, for example, is one of the most disruptive of the emotions and feeds on itself.

Here are six ways anxiety affects you mentally:

Anxiety is distracting. You cannot focus your mind fully on two things at once. When you need to pay attention to a certain play you can't be worrying about the last one or the one coming next. But if you are anxious, you are more likely to focus your mind on the anxiety than on the task at hand, since the anxiety—with all the body feelings it stimulates—tends to be more compelling.

Let's say, for example, you have bowled six good frames. You are enjoying yourself. But just before you step up for the seventh frame, your opponent says, "You're really playing over your head, champ! Keep it up and you're liable to break 200."

Right away you feel twinges of emotion. You might feel embarrassed. You might also feel a little angry at your opponent's attempt to ruffle you. Now, you should be concentrating on the alley, the pins, and your moves, of course. But it's hard to shut off imagination and, stimulated by emotional response, you may start thinking, *I'll show him!* And so you may even gutter the ball.

Anxiety can be hypnotic. What makes worrisome ideas so potent is the fact that you feel their physical effects almost at the same instant they enter your mind. This is why it is so easy to be carried away by a fear, and unwittingly make that about which you are tense happen. If a golfer is particularly bothered by a water hazard on a certain hole, for example, a familiar experience is for him to hit the ball right where he feared it would go—into the drink. His fear of the hazard causes him to focus on what could go wrong rather than on what he has to do to make the shot go right. Without knowing it, he probably lined himself up with the hazard and aimed there instead of beyond it, and his muscles, which were only doing their job, responded to what was on his mind—which was hypnotized by emotion.

A baseball player once told me he made an error—not adjusting his fielder's position for a left-handed batter—and the error was exactly what he had worried might happen. The anxiety about doing something wrong so preoccupied him that it prevented him from concentrating on getting himself into the correct position. He had actually set up the error he was so frightened of making.

Anxiety can ruin strategy and tactical judgment. A baseball player who is not a home run hitter can strike out going for the fences in a clutch situation, because in his overeagerness he forgets that he is a good hitter who could more easily have gotten a single. A weekend tennis player can feel inferior because he doesn't have a strong serve and so not take advantage of his good volleying ability, failing to realize that even some tennis greats (such as Ken Rosewall and Jimmy Connors) have succeeded without the big serve. Anxiety, then, tends to make you react to your emotions rather than to the situation, and you become a victim of your weaknesses instead of building a strategy around your strong points. Fear of failure can make you prematurely panic that your strategy isn't working, and lead you to shift willy-nilly from one strategy to another. Likewise, intimidation can seize your attention and trap you into playing your opponent's game, prohibiting you from formulating effective tactics for playing your own game.

Anxiety creates avoidance and halts development. Anxiety can do more than temporarily wreck your concentration; it can arrest the development of your skills and affect your overall attitude toward your game. Anxiety is unpleasant and the resulting poor performance leads to more anxiety and unpleasant feelings. Since it is natural to avoid what is unpleasurable, you can develop an aversion for attempting certain types of shots, for example, because you don't do them well and want to avoid frustration. The trouble is, of course, that if you ever want to improve a shot, you have to practice it more, not less. But avoidance is a common problem. I know several tennis players whose anxiety over their net game makes them avoid playing the net at all costs; so even when the situation really demands net play, they lack both the will and the skill for it.

Anxiety makes you stop trying. If the frustration cycle isn't broken, you begin to despair of improvement. It's a defense against feeling depressed: "I'm no good, so I should face it."

For some players this becomes so agonizing, they quit sports entirely. After frustrating, embarrassing experiences with athletics in childhood, they want no further part of it. "I'm simply not athletic," they say. What they really are saying is: Who needs aggravation, anxiety, and ridicule?

What's sad is that all the mental anguish doesn't need to be part of the sports experience. In fact, the best way to improve athletic performance is to dump the negative emotional baggage and concentrate on what makes athletics pleasurable. Often the carrot works better than the stick. One of my graduate students, Harvey Loew, found this out when he studied the effects of different coaching approaches on the running performance of junior high school students. The runners were divided into five groups. One group was praised after it had run, no matter how well each person did; one group received no comments at all; the third group was criticized; and the last two groups received both praise and criticism in reverse order. It developed that the group that got *only* praise improved its time the most.

One incident in the study struck me as particularly poignant. A runner in the "praise group" who was overweight and ran slowly, after being praised several times, turned to the experimenter and said, "What's wrong with you? Don't you know I'm slow? Why do you keep saying nice things to me?" The boy is typical of many youths and many adults who as children had bad experiences with sports; they feel they're no good or don't deserve any praise because they don't live up to some imaginary high standard. Indeed, because of the premium society places on exceptional athletic talent, *most* people feel left out. They don't feel worthy enough to work with the talents they *do* have and thus fail to develop their own real potential.

Anxiety can make you sick. Many players develop psychosomatic problems in response to the pressure to perform. Some consistently overexert themselves in training, weakening and even hurting themselves in an effort to prove their self-worth or, unconsciously, to avoid having to face the test of the actual game. They may not be as competitive as they feel society demands they be, but they can't admit this to themselves. So they get themselves off the hook by developing an injury.

I remember discussing the case of a pro football player with his trainer, who could not understand why the player always developed a crippling back pain several times during a season. We determined that the pain occurred before games with certain teams in which the player would have to face certain outstanding athletes. The pain was real enough to the player, despite its psychosomatic origins, but it also was his defense against a fear that he felt he couldn't admit on a conscious level. He felt he could not work successfully against the opponent, and so the best option was to pull out—to quit.

It is not the intrinsic challenges of sports that do most of the damage. It is the exaggeration of pressures that causes us to suffer far more anxiety than is warranted. Such disproportionate social and personal pressures to perform—especially as felt by most recreational athletes—end up defeating their own purpose. What, then, is the answer? It lies in your ability to channel your emotions and control your own game. And the first step toward that is to do a scouting report on yourself.

THE SPORTS EMOTIONAL-REACTION PROFILE:
Scouting Yourself

Our psychological tendencies can help or hinder us depending on how much we possess them or they possess us.

Golfer Dave Stockton was once asked at the start of a Masters' tournament to name the player he most feared in that field of golf champions.

"Me," he answered without hesitation.

No one has ever stated more succinctly the truth that it's what goes on inside you that counts most in athletic performance.

The first order of business in controlling the psychological side of your game is to become aware of it. I am talking here about normal psychological problems we all face in sports. My purpose is to help you to simply become more aware of your particular emotional problems in athletics, not to cure you of some terrible neurosis. I am not your shrink. I am not offering any diagnoses or cures for mental disorders. We will not try to take apart your character and examine it under a microscope. The goal of self-scouting is simply to help you build up your self-awareness so that you can use it as a tool to keep emotional problems from getting out of hand and spoiling your game.

Professional teams go to great lengths to scout opponents and team prospects. They also continually scout themselves, scrupulously recording every play and analyzing their own strengths and weaknesses. Every player of every pro football team, for example, on the Tuesday following a game goes over the event play by play. Recreational athletes, on the other hand, don't go in for much self-searching. Most people are simply not all that self-analytical, don't have the techniques to do it, and are perhaps afraid that holding up a mirror to themselves will point out shortcomings they'd just as soon not be reminded of. Thus, ashamed of not doing as well as we think society demands of us, we play on with an ignorance-is-bliss attitude, making the same mistakes again and again and wondering why.

The reason we feel this way is that most of us confuse scouting our own game with *sitting in judgment* of ourselves, and we think we already have sufficient evidence in the score of our games to make that judgment. But scores are not what I mean by self-scouting. The object of self-scouting is not to look back but to look forward and to build. Thus, what we want is for you to get as much precise, specific, *non*judgmental information about yourself as possible. With this kind of information we are able to move beyond self-defeating generalizations—toward pinpointing problems and understanding what is causing them.

The kind of scouting report we're looking for is not "I just can't seem to get my game together," but might be something as follows: "I become too easily intimidated a) when facing certain players and b) if early in the game I fall behind. My lack of assertiveness makes me perform below my potential, which makes me angry with myself, which in turn makes me more nervous and interferes with my performance. To break this cycle, I need to be aware of my reactions and not allow them to interfere with my concentration."

To help you gain this kind of information I am presenting two self-scouting methods for getting you in better touch with your game. The first is the Sports Emotional-Reaction Profile (SERP), which will map out your basic psychological tendencies in sports. The second (Chapter 7) is the Physical Self-Scouting Survey, which puts your physical performance in perspective by breaking it down into components.

Now for the SERP.

THE SPORTS EMOTIONAL- REACTION PROFILE

Self-awareness is the first step toward being in better control of your own game.

No one type of personality is better suited to athletics than another. Consider the world's two greatest home-run hitters: Babe Ruth was flamboyant and irascible; Hank Aaron is soft-spoken and introverted. One's particular personality, however, has its advantages and its disadvantages in coping with the various stress situations in sports, and that's what we hope to determine from your Sports Emotional-Reaction Profile. The SERP creates an outline of your traits by helping you find out your emotional reactions to your game, what in sports you find most compelling, what triggers the most active responses. It is designed to be self-scored—you are your own scout here.

Above all don't consider it to be a "test." There are no right or wrong answers. You are using it only as a tool to seek information about yourself. Remember, by becoming more familiar with your particular psychological tendencies in sports, you will be better able to defuse potential emotional problems and feel at ease with yourself at play.

Here is how the SERP works. Listed below are some common feelings or attitudes concerning athletic performance. Read each item carefully and check the scale to the right indicating how frequently the item conforms to your personal experience in athletics. (The scale is fairly subjective, but "Almost Always" means the experience happens about 90 percent of the time, "Often" means about 75 percent, "Sometimes" means about 50 percent, "Seldom" about 25 percent, and "Almost Never" about 10 percent.) Think each statement over and try to be as accurate as

---

QUESTIONS FOR SPORTS EMOTIONAL-REACTION PROFILE

1. I do not consider my playing worthwhile unless I'm near my best.

2. I am intimidated by aggressive players.

3. Little annoyances can throw me off my game.

4. I can get my mind to be calm during a game.

5. I have faith in my ability.

6. I apologize to others when I make a mistake or play poorly.

7. I organize my strategy before playing.

8. I play primarily for fun.

9. I speak out whenever I have something to say in an athletic contest.

10. I have nerves of steel during a game.

11. I make more mistakes during the pressure part of a game.

12. I lack confidence in my game.

13. I avoid looking at what I have done wrong.

possible. This survey can be useful only if you base your responses on what you *actually feel* or what you *actually do*. Do not answer on the basis of how you believe you *should* feel or how you think others feel about you.

You may want to psych out the test to look good or to try to beat it. If you do, you are beating yourself, not improving.

Okay, are you ready? Stop reading and get a pencil. This book will have less value if you keep on going and read the scoring and interpretation material. I urge you to take the SERP—right now.

Feel free to mark directly in this book. It will make it your personal psychological athletic diary.

	ALMOST ALWAYS	OFTEN	SOMETIMES	SELDOM	ALMOST NEVER
1.	_____	_____	_____	_____	_____
2.	_____	_____	_____	_____	_____
3.	_____	_____	_____	_____	_____
4.	_____	_____	_____	_____	_____
5.	_____	_____	_____	_____	_____
6.	_____	_____	_____	_____	_____
7.	_____	_____	_____	_____	_____
8.	_____	_____	_____	_____	_____
9.	_____	_____	_____	_____	_____
10.	_____	_____	_____	_____	_____
11.	_____	_____	_____	_____	_____
12.	_____	_____	_____	_____	_____
13.	_____	_____	_____	_____	_____

SERP QUESTIONS (continued)

14. I play spontaneously rather than having a game plan in mind.

15. I want to be the best on the playing field.

16. I laugh things off rather than get angry about them.

17. I am influenced by what others think about my athletic performances.

18. I can control my nervousness during a game.

19. I expect to win before a contest.

20. My mistakes make me feel bad for days.

21. I have a routine that I adhere to when I practice or play.

22. I prefer to play with people who do not make the game a "contest."

23. I am a "take charge" type of performer.

24. I am "emotionally numb" during a game.

25. My nervousness interferes with my game.

26. I think about losing a game even before it begins.

27. I think about the errors my opponent may make rather than play my own game.

28. I jump from one thing to another trying to improve my game.

29. I don't feel like playing unless I have a challenge.

30. When my opponents show anger, I try not to pay any attention.

31. An offhand comment by someone can ruin my game.

32. I enjoy the pressure part of a game because I do well.

33. I like to challenge the tougher opponents.

34. I worry about my failures more than I enjoy my successes.

35. I try to find ways to be more efficient at my game.

	ALMOST ALWAYS	OFTEN	SOMETIMES	SELDOM	ALMOST NEVER
14.					
15.					
16.					
17.					
18.					
19.					
20.					
21.					
22.					
23.					
24.					
25.					
26.					
27.					
28.					
29.					
30.					
31.					
32.					
33.					
34.					
35.					

SERP QUESTIONS (continued)

36. I can enjoy playing a game while making a lot of mistakes.

37. I am assertive on the athletic field.

38. I try to block everything out of my mind during a contest.

39. I worry about getting into tight spots long before they occur.

40. I worry that my opponents will humiliate me.

41. I try to avoid thinking about my mistakes.

42. I don't know what I am going to do until a game gets underway.

SCORING THE SERP

Identifying your psychological characteristics.

At this point it should be stated that the main thrust of the Sports Emotional-Reaction Profile, for now, is simply self-awareness. We are not at the moment concerned with straightening out difficulties, if any; that will come later. Now what we are trying to do is simply identify the outstanding psychological characteristics of your athletic behavior.

The forty-two items in the SERP cover seven separate psychological areas having a bearing on athletics. They are: *Desire, Assertiveness, Sensitivity, Tension Control, Confidence, Personal Accountability,* and *Self-Discipline.* There are six items devoted to each of the seven areas. Of these, three describe the area in a positive way and three show a negative outlook. For example, item 7, which relates to Self-Discipline, poses that area in a *positive* direction by stating, "I organize my strategy before playing." Item 28,

	ALMOST ALWAYS	OFTEN	SOMETIMES	SELDOM	ALMOST NEVER
36.	_____	_____	_____	_____	_____
37.	_____	_____	_____	_____	_____
38.	_____	_____	_____	_____	_____
39.	_____	_____	_____	_____	_____
40.	_____	_____	_____	_____	_____
41.	_____	_____	_____	_____	_____
42.	_____	_____	_____	_____	_____

which also relates to Self-Discipline, puts it in a *negative* way, saying, "I jump from one thing to another trying to improve my game."

Now, here's how to score your answers to the questions:

Positive items. All items indicated as *positive* are scored as follows:

Almost Always	5 points
Often	4 points
Sometimes	3 points
Seldom	2 points
Almost Never	1 point

Negative items. All items indicated as *negative* are scored the reverse, as follows:

Almost Always	1 point
Often	2 points
Sometimes	3 points
Seldom	4 points
Almost Never	5 points

Read through the following scoring table for each of the seven psychological areas.

Beneath each area the *left-hand* column shows the question-item number.

The other columns indicate the score of the response you checked. For instance, if for Item 1 you checked "Seldom," that response is worth 2 points. If for Item 41 you checked "Seldom," that response is worth 4 points.

See how you answered each question on the survey, and *circle* the points for each response you made.

There are six entries for each psychological area. To obtain your *total score* for each area, total up the six scores you've circled.

DESIRE:

ITEM NO.	ALMOST ALWAYS	OFTEN	SOMETIMES	SELDOM	ALMOST NEVER
1	5	4	3	2	1
15	5	4	3	2	1
29	5	4	3	2	1
8	1	2	3	4	5
22	1	2	3	4	5
36	1	2	3	4	5

Total Score for Desire: _____

ASSERTIVENESS:

ITEM NO.	ALMOST ALWAYS	OFTEN	SOMETIMES	SELDOM	ALMOST NEVER
9	5	4	3	2	1
23	5	4	3	2	1
37	5	4	3	2	1
2	1	2	3	4	5
16	1	2	3	4	5
30	1	2	3	4	5

Total Score for Assertiveness: _____

SENSITIVITY:

ITEM NO.	ALMOST ALWAYS	OFTEN	SOMETIMES	SELDOM	ALMOST NEVER
3	5	4	3	2	1
17	5	4	3	2	1
31	5	4	3	2	1
10	1	2	3	4	5
24	1	2	3	4	5
38	1	2	3	4	5

Total Score for Sensitivity: _____

TENSION CONTROL:

ITEM NO.	ALMOST ALWAYS	OFTEN	SOMETIMES	SELDOM	ALMOST NEVER
4	5	4	3	2	1
18	5	4	3	2	1
32	5	4	3	2	1

TENSION CONTROL (continued)

ITEM NUMBER		POSITIVE OR NEGATIVE		YOUR SCORE
11	1	2	3	4	5
25	1	2	3	4	5
39	1	2	3	4	5

Total Score for Tension Control: _____

CONFIDENCE:

ITEM NO.	ALMOST ALWAYS	OFTEN	SOMETIMES	SELDOM	ALMOST NEVER
5	5	4	3	2	1
19	5	4	3	2	1
33	5	4	3	2	1
12	1	2	3	4	5
26	1	2	3	4	5
40	1	2	3	4	5

Total Score for Confidence: _____

PERSONAL ACCOUNTABILITY:

ITEM NO.	ALMOST ALWAYS	OFTEN	SOMETIMES	SELDOM	ALMOST NEVER
6	5	4	3	2	1
20	5	4	3	2	1
34	5	4	3	2	1
13	1	2	3	4	5
27	1	2	3	4	5
41	1	2	3	4	5

Total Score for Personal Accountability: _____

SELF-DISCIPLINE:

ITEM NO.	ALMOST ALWAYS	OFTEN	SOMETIMES	SELDOM	ALMOST NEVER
7	5	4	3	2	1
21	5	4	3	2	1
35	5	4	3	2	1
14	1	2	3	4	5
28	1	2	3	4	5
42	1	2	3	4	5

Total Score for Self-Discipline: _____

TRANSLATING YOUR SCORE INTO YOUR PROFILE

Drawing your psychological graph.

The total score for each of the seven psychological areas can be as low as 5 and as high as 30. A high score (25-30) or low score (5-10) in an area *may* signal difficulties, but not necessarily—it depends on the psychological area, as we shall see in the next chapter. In any case, there is no onus to being high or low in any area, since each area has different assets and liabilities.

Now translate your total score in each of the areas onto the blank graph on page 58. This psychological graph will give you a visual profile of your emotional reactions in athletics in these seven areas. To show you a sample of how such profiles can look, I have presented the SERPs for myself and my coauthor, Umberto Tosi.

TUTKO'S SERP

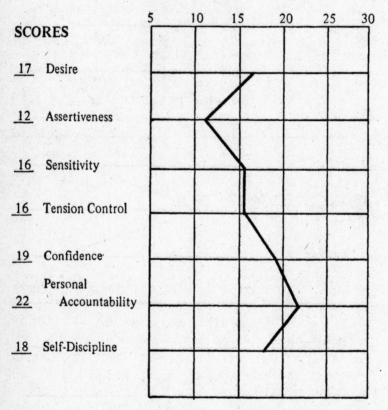

SCORES

17 Desire

12 Assertiveness

16 Sensitivity

16 Tension Control

19 Confidence

22 Personal
      Accountability

18 Self-Discipline

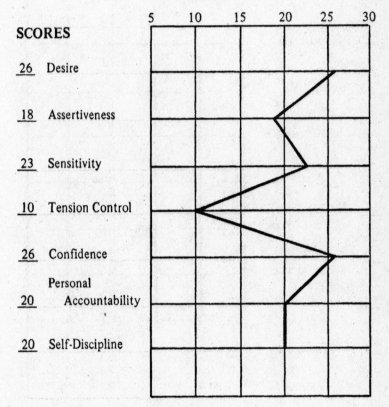

TOSI'S SERP

SCORES

26 Desire

18 Assertiveness

23 Sensitivity

10 Tension Control

26 Confidence

20 Personal Accountability

20 Self-Discipline

YOUR SPORTS EMOTIONAL-REACTION PROFILE

**YOUR
SCORES**

	5	10	15	20	25	30

___ Desire

___ Assertiveness

___ Sensitivity

___ Tension Control

___ Confidence

Personal
___   Accountability

___ Self-Discipline

Now that you know what your Sports Emotional-Reaction Profile is, let us analyze, in the next chapter, what the high and low scores mean.

6

SCORING YOURSELF:
What Your Profile Means

Taking a look at the scouting report.

No doubt you have a general understanding of the meaning of each of the seven psychological traits you scored on your profile—Desire, Assertiveness, Sensitivity, Tension Control, Confidence, Personal Accountability, and Self-Discipline—but I will define the terms more strictly, as they apply to sports, as I explain what the scores mean.

A trait is likely to be an asset to your game if your SERP score on it falls within a certain acceptable range. Scores outside that range, however, may mean the trait is a hindrance to your performance. By checking your scores against the definitions and analyses below you can begin to spot difficulties. Extreme low and high scores (under 10 and over 25) indicate areas to which you should give special attention. But, depending on the area, as we shall explain, even scores between 10 and 25 can signify difficulties, if the line on your graph bends toward the high or the low.

Of course, a high or low score doesn't mean that trait is *necessarily* a problem. You have to make that judgment for yourself—as I said, you are your own coach here. Indeed, you may not care that your score is high or low on a particular trait. I once told a pro coach after we had scored his Athletic Motivation Inventory that he was very high on drive—that in fact only 5 percent of the population was more driven than he. He immediately corrected me by saying that *nobody* was more driven than he—and that he didn't feel it was a problem.

I suggest you read all categories, since few of us act totally one way or another in these behavioral areas. (It is possible to be appropriately confident most of the time and overconfident some of the time; indeed, your Sports Emotional-Reaction Profile could vary somewhat were you to do it a few months from now or after having won or lost a game.)

The chapter is set up as follows: There is a general description of each psychological trait, comments on the possible meanings of a high or low score, and (where these present a problem) the typical comments made by people with those scores, common behavior they exhibit, and ways of handling the situation. The "typical comments," in particular, represent the little internal voice, the ultimate Monday-morning quarterback who is always telling us what we should have done to make our play more perfect; when you hear it, you know your psychological game is interfering with your physical game.

Now let's evaluate your scores.

1. DESIRE

Desire is the personal push in athletics, the drive for success, the striving for excellence. Desire can be a measure of trying to *be the best* or to *do your best*.

Scores between 5 and 25 indicate you are generally realistic in setting the goals you strive for. The higher the score, the more push you have toward achieving those goals. The lower the score, the more content you are with your game as is.

Low Score (5-10): "I Don't Care"

A low score on desire is generally not a problem. If one is a player who genuinely doesn't care that much about athletic achievement and just enjoys getting out for the fresh air and exercise, then there is no conflict to create anxiety and disturb his ability to play.

A lack of desire in sports is only a problem if it stems from a person's fear that trying harder is bound to result in failure. However, our experience with this kind of player is minimal, since athlete testing procedures are not aimed at people who don't give a damn.

High Score (25-30): The Perfectionist

Desire is fine as long as you can control it. Sometimes it controls you. The main problem with the Perfectionist is that he is never content with his performance because he is always, as it were, in a personal Super Bowl contest, always trying for the perfect game. He tends to become impatient with himself, to demand too much, to measure himself against too high a standard, to ignore improvements and dwell on his shortcomings instead of evaluating the game in its own context.

Much of what the Perfectionist does is self-defeating. He wants to improve performance, but ironically, by setting overly ambitious goals, he sets himself up for constant anxiety. The tensions thus created interfere with the very performance he wants to perfect.

Typical Comments. Here are some typical expressions the Perfectionist says to himself or others: "I'm doing okay, but I'm no Johnny Miller yet." "I won, but I should have beaten that guy in straight sets." "My game is way off." "Come on, you can do better than that!" (to himself).

Common Behavior. A perfectionist will take up a sport and be disappointed after only a few lessons that his performance doesn't match that of far more experienced players. If the Perfectionist does well, this only raises expectations. For example, a perfectionist bowler will get three strikes in a row and then expect a strike the next time, too, even though three strikes may be his best ever performance. Once he has attained something it seems to lose its glamour. If he becomes so good in the B league that he makes the A league, he doesn't congratulate himself—rather, he becomes depressed at his newly acquired low ranking in the A league. Even if he wins a game, he worries about things he did wrong that almost cost him the contest, and vows to work harder on those areas. He will quit a game entirely, disgusted at not achieving his goals. This drive toward perfection also can steer a player toward ruthlessness, especially toward teammates who may not be so driven themselves.

The Perfectionist goes in for endless hours of practice and an unswerving dedication to winning. He will try all sorts of new equipment, impatiently moving from one type to another when the new gear doesn't seem to provide enough improvement. He keeps up on all the latest skill techniques and pesters more successful (winning) players for their "secrets." When he watches games on television, he identifies with the champions, but is very critical, almost feels betrayed, when his team blows it. He sometimes blows games himself by pushing too hard on all fronts, rather than gearing his strategy around the plusses and minuses of his abilities. Sprains and other injuries are an increased threat to perfectionist athletes, who tend to go beyond what their physical condition permits.

Handling the Situation. The Perfectionist should reevaluate not only his specific goals in a sport but the basic reasons he participates as well. Frequently, his problems are an extension of what he is trying to do in daily life—on the job, for instance. One may be an extremely competitive person in business and be carrying this over into his game. He should remind himself he is probably not playing just for the challenge of competition alone, but also as a means of relaxation and recreation to refresh himself for the challenges he faces at work.

The Perfectionist needs to think realistically about his athletic talents and about how much he *really* is willing to give to improve them. If, like most recreational athletes, he doesn't want to spend ten hours a day practicing, going through the kind of grueling workouts required of those whose careers are in athletics, then he should set his expectations of himself accordingly, keeping them in line with the talent and time he has to give to what is really only a game.

It may at first seem like some kind of self-betrayal to "lower your standards," but in reality the setting of impossible goals does not improve performance and only kills pleasure. An athlete must set goals that are commensurate with *his* talents, not based upon what others do. (In the next chapter, you will have an opportunity to do this by scouting your physical performance.)

In actual play a good way of containing perfectionist problems is to concentrate more on individual plays, as they are executed, rather than always on the final score. This refocuses one's attention away from far-off goals, so that instead of being under pressure to achieve some fantastic score at the end of the game, one's mind is on the play at hand. This, paradoxically, will help the score in the long run.

Because the Perfectionist is often unconscious of what he expects of himself and is unaware of the unrealistic goals he has set, he would do well to seriously think about, prior to a game, what his specific goals and expectations are. Otherwise, during the game, he will continue to change his goals, so that if he does well in the beginning, he will set his standards even higher, and if he does poorly in the beginning, he will become disillusioned with the whole game. The thing to keep in mind is the fact that no one can play the game without error, that even the very best players *constantly* make mistakes. Even Jimmy Connors sometimes double-faults, and Jack Nicklaus hits the ball into the lake.

2. ASSERTIVENESS

Assertiveness is feeling that you can do something about your game to bring about change. The assertive player does not use alibis when he is not doing well. Rather, he says to himself, "My drive isn't long enough; I'm going to have to practice to strengthen that area." The assertive player also does not allow other players to take advantage of him by setting a game pace with which he is not comfortable or by continually talking if the talk distracts him. In addition, assertiveness is indicated by one's taking appropriate risks and not always taking the easier way out. For example, in bowling it might mean going for a difficult split rather than settling for a single pin. In tennis, it might mean trying to make a strong second serve rather than just trying to put the ball into play. Healthy assertiveness involves knowing one's own limits and bending when necessary, but not allowing either the players or the difficulty of the game to determine how one plays. If you score between 10 and 25 in this area you tend to show healthy assertiveness in most sports situations.

Low Score (5-10): The Intimidated

Athletes scoring low on assertiveness are intimidated too easily, sometimes feeling they are beaten even before they start. More assertive players take control, and the Caspar Milquetoasts find themselves playing their adversary's game. Intimidated players typically react to a problem by simply withdrawing from the game, rather than confronting the difficulty and risking failure.

Many individuals who are low in assertiveness are fearful of their own anger, of what they might do to others if they let loose. Rather than explode, they become sponges, absorbing the anger of others. With some people it can even get to the point where they view winning as being *too* assertive, and so losing becomes an unconsciously promoted behavior which allows them not to threaten their opponent. Others are easily intimidated because of feelings of personal inadequacy. They sell themselves short and believe it would be no contest if they did try to assert themselves.

When playing against someone who is very good, the nonassertive player generally plays less well than he does ordinarily because he is afraid that challenging the better player will get him irritated so that he will *really* beat the Intimidated one. Similarly, if there is verbal aggression of any kind during the match, Intimidated is silent for fear that anything he says might make the other player especially mad at him.

Nonassertiveness is particularly a problem with women in sports, since being assertive is contrary to the stereotypical role women are taught. This is often seen in a game in which men and women are participating simultaneously, where the psychological pressures on a woman are especially strong.

Women who have overcome the assertiveness problem in athletics, therefore, tend to be very much better than other female players, who may be equally talented physically but always holding back psychologically.

Typical Comments. "These guys are rough." "Nice shot" (said to opponent too often). "Hey, take it easy!" "This golf course is too tough for me."

Common Behavior. Intimidated athletes tend to avoid head-on challenges, especially from aggressive players. As might be expected, they shy away from physical contact sports, and in the sports they do play they rarely argue a disputed point. If an opponent makes a sensational shot, they feel a terrible sense of inadequacy. As spectators they tend to root for underdogs, sometimes making unwise bets.

A big problem with such athletes is that they may too readily accept subordinate roles that others may hang on them. For example, one might start playing tennis regularly with more skilled players who initially accept him as lowest in the pecking order—as a doubles partner, say, but not someone to be taken seriously in a singles match. Accepting this vision of his capabilities, a player might unconsciously stop trying to improve his skills and even overlook easy corrections of his technique.

When the Intimidated gets ahead of his opponent, he tends to ease off and sometimes lets games slip away from him, making himself angry for letting it happen. This in turn may lead him to dream about revenge—in the classic Charles Atlas example, to yearn to get back at the guy who kicked sand in his face—but inevitably, when the time comes, he lets it happen again.

Handling the Situation. To convert his fear of being intimidated into productive behavior, the first thing an underassertive athlete must do is determine specifically when he feels intimidated and what specifically his opponent is doing that triggers that feeling. One clue to this feeling is that it is frequently accompanied by a fear of speaking out. For instance, if after having done something well, one is afraid to display his pleasure because it might make his opponent play harder, then one is intimidated. The next step is to weigh the consequences of being assertive in return. Many find that fear of others is more threatening than the consequences of not being assertive. But if an opponent is trying to browbeat you, it is reasonable to let him know that his behavior is annoying. If you are afraid to assert yourself in your game, you can try to practice it. For instance, going to a driving range and hitting a bucket of golf balls hard enough to practically rip the covers off (and not worry about where the balls go, since this is a psychological exercise) may get you moving away from a shy, overly cautious game.

A major area of intimidation is the fear of being beaten in a contact sport like basketball or football or even at the net in a volleyball game. This fear is so great that many players, even good players, are not where they should be during the course of the action because they fear if they are there they may be both hurt physically and beaten by opposing players. To become more assertive, a player should set as his goal simply to *be* at the place where the action is. Then, as he overcomes his fear of being in the action, he can begin to perform more effectively during it. This works equally well whether one is trying to develop his rebounding ability in basketball or take to the net more in tennis.

High Score (25-30): The Killer

Overassertiveness can be a greater problem than underassertiveness because it manifests itself as hostility and misspent energy. I encountered a prime example of this several years ago when I counseled a pro football team. One player was so assertive that he had become a detriment to the team. It seemed that his only reason for playing was to hit. In one game when his team was trying to put together a last-chance drive in the closing minutes of play, he was penalized on two consecutive plays for unsportsmanlike conduct. Both penalties were for clipping—the first time for doing it on a player who was already out of bounds, and the second time for doing it after the whistle had blown! At that time you could describe this man as "a fight waiting for some place to happen." Only after much counseling did he finally realize his assertiveness had gotten out of hand and become destructive.

Preoccupation with one's personal hostilities often leads to poor strategy and can make a player needlessly vulnerable. Other players may take advantage of his overaggressiveness, drawing him into playing the blindly charging bull while they play the matador. In the 1974 Muhammad Ali-George Foreman heavyweight fight in Zaire, Ali conserved his energy through most of the rounds by staying on the ropes, at the same time luring and taunting Foreman into dogged and exhausting pursuit. Ali let Foreman wear himself out, then made his move and knocked him out. Foreman's mistake, Ali pointed out afterward, was in trying too hard for the knockout in every round rather than pacing himself.

If you are inclined to be short-tempered and overly aggressive, you may see your sports participation as a continual fight—a savage battle rather than an enjoyable challenge. Your anger may not only manifest itself physically, but (as we shall see later in the chapter on psych-outs) also verbally, inviting remarks, insults, and snide comments which will alienate you from your partners and even your friends.

Most overassertiveness really is defensive. It occurs because we interpret what is happening as threatening and feel we must strike back. We fear defeat in an exaggerated way, as if it would mean personal humiliation, and we dish it back out in kind, trying to humble the enemy. If someone is threatening your survival, it's natural to be angry. But the anger then can take control of you, affecting your performance and leading to more feelings of humiliation and anger as you play poorly.

Typical Comments. "I'm going to ram this one down his gullet." "Come on, let's get going!" "Better look out; I'm coming after you." "You're taking too much time." "That got him."

Common Behavior. Killer types want to be in charge of all situations and tend to become nervous when luck, or an opponent on a hot streak, goes against them. They tend to be too easily provoked, sometimes into costly mistakes, and try to shove the ball down their opponents' throats even when a soft shot would be better. They tend to be very physical if they play contact sports, and as spectators tend to root for the physical, grind-'em-out teams. They will make a big point of a disputed call or play. Since they may be unable to enjoy a game they can't totally dominate, they may seek out competition that is too easy to give them any real challenge, thus cutting off the opportunity to sharpen their skills.

Other players may see them as being too pushy, even obnoxious. The Killer athlete may make them angry enough to do their best to try to beat him. Jimmy Connors has said that he plays better when he feels everyone is against him, but few of us enjoy the pressures of that kind of role, even if we feel compelled to play it.

The overly aggressive player may also feel obligated to try

to rattle the opposition with insults, either subtle or obvious. This may indeed win him a game, but it doesn't make him any friends and certainly causes him to lose one of the prime values of recreational sports, namely, the sociability.

As a Killer fan, the overly aggressive athlete can be heard yelling "Murder him!" from the stands. Indeed, these kinds of statements have become part of our athletic vocabulary and this seems to give social sanction to the most aggressive kind of behavior on the playing field. Almost every professional hockey team has one player known as the "enforcer" or the "policeman" because of his readiness to fight or to check savagely to avenge attacks on his teammates. Such terms can even go beyond mere characterization and become inextricably linked to a player's real name—witness Mean Joe Greene. Certainly when it means the ability to pull yourself together for an important point or not to let up when you're ahead, the killer instinct is essential. However, when it means playing every point as if your life depended on it, for the recreational player, all the killer instinct kills is the pleasure of the game.

Handling the Situation. The main thing the overly aggressive person has to do is get control of his anger. To do this he can use the positive side of assertiveness he already has—that he is active, not passive, and wants to take charge of the situation. What he needs is to take a little time to stop and think before his anger can gain the upper hand. This allows him time to cool down and to think about the game in a less dramatic context, to shake off the feelings of being threatened, and to refocus attention on the challenge of the next play. The best way to do this is to devise a ritual to go through whenever anger starts taking over. For example, one may say something specifically nonaggressive to himself under his breath, count, plan strategy, or perform a series of body movements between plays. We will explain some of these in the chapters on Sports Psyching.

3. SENSITIVITY

Healthy sensitivity in athletics is the ability to get pleasure—indeed, elation and energy—from our successful plays, without being overly distressed when we make mistakes or even a series of mistakes. It is the ability to adjust to others or the conditions around us. If your score is between 10 and 25, you are within a productive sensitivity range—you are sensitive to what is happening around you but emotionally resilient enough to cope with adverse outside conditions.

Low Score (5-10): The Stonewaller

In general, a low score is not a problem because it means that few elements outside of the game affect how one plays. Such an athlete thus has a great deal of emotional resilience, which, of course, is an asset in sports competition. However, this type of player may be so singleminded and thick-skinned that other players may see him as being insensitive and indifferent—even though he may see himself as an underdog, valiantly hanging tough.

Typical Comments. "Those knuckleheads don't know what they're doing" (about teammates). "I'm going to have to start calling the shots around here." "What does the coach know? He hasn't been on a court in fifteen years." "No, no, no, not that way! Let me show you." "I'm not going to take a penalty on this hole; I'll just play it out." "It's just a sprain; I can play all right." "Oh, come on, it isn't that dark yet; let's hit a few more."

Common Behavior. Sometimes this player puts himself behind the eight ball. He may see himself as a perpetual underdog, a second-half player who performs best when he comes from behind and may indeed arrange to put himself in that position. He may not have much confidence in himself early in a game, or simply figure he doesn't have to try hard because he can make it up later, but whatever the cause, he risks getting so far in the hole he can't get out. As a spectator, he may root for teams with the longest odds.

Handling the Situation. Obviously, one who is low on Sensitivity should pay more attention to the early stages of his game and learn to focus on each play as it happens. He should learn, in other words, to play at the opening of a contest as he would toward the end—after all, the action he has to accomplish is the same whether the score says he is ahead or behind. Emotional resilience is a valuable asset. But it needs to be thought of as insurance rather than as a crutch. In addition, the Insensitive should keep an ear open to what his teammates and instructor or coach are saying, since by setting himself up as an expert he may be depriving himself of the cooperation of other team members and the expert advice that he needs to win.

High Score (25-30):
The Supersensitive

One may be so sensitive that he becomes easily distracted by external stimuli, and constantly reacts to the atmosphere around him. The overly sensitive athlete is therefore easily psyched by other players. *Their* activity and *their* game become more important than how he is performing himself.

I remember counseling an outstanding collegiate football player who was seriously thinking about not trying out for the pros even though he had already been picked as a high draft choice by a desirable team. His reason was that he'd heard the coach of the team that had drafted him was highly critical of his players and yelled a great deal. He said that when a coach acted in this gruff manner, his mind would automatically shut out the content of what was being said and he would only see the coach as being extremely angry and disappointed with him. He would not respond to the factual messages, only the emotional ones. The player did join the team, but it took a full season of counseling him, along with some patient cooperation on the part of the coach, for him to get over these feelings of alienation and be able to roll with the emotional punches.

To the Supersensitive, a bad shot, a bad bounce of the ball, an adverse ruling, a teammate mildly disappointed at his performance, an opponent gloating at his setbacks—all are felt as personal affronts. This makes it difficult for him to recover if he falls behind.

Typical Comments. "You really know how to hurt a guy." "That's it, there goes my score" (after a missed play). "The other guys must think I'm terrible." "This is embarrassing." "I'm really going to look stupid if I miss." "I hope the weather will be warm." "Give me a break, will you?"

Common Behavior. The Supersensitive becomes discouraged quickly and often thinks himself a first-half player who must pile up points early in order to win. This, of course, puts pressure on him at the start, and the result is that when things don't go right early he begins to think his best won't be good enough, so he folds. When others attempt to help him with specific advice, he regards what they say with suspicion. Critical comments, even made in fun, can shake him badly and break his concentration.

The Supersensitive is very self-conscious. He feels all eyes on him when he steps up to the plate, the tee, or the service line. If he is leading in a game, he may feel sorry for the other players. If he is behind, he may feel belittled. Often he'll react by pouting, or giving up trying when things go wrong. If he makes a great shot, he expects other players to compliment him. When he makes a mistake, he feels everyone is secretly thinking about what a poor player he is. He's upset when a team he is rooting for gets some bad breaks. When the other team intercepts and gets ahead by a touchdown, even if it's only still in the first half, he may think, "Well, it's all over now; we'll never win."

Handling the Situation. To sort himself out, the Supersensitive must learn to separate facts from overly emotional responses to those facts. The emotional message may be, "I blew it, I'm no good," but if one looks at the facts he will find it is something he may be able to correct on the next play. Missing a shot may be due to some wrong move, wrong stance, or other error in technique.

Some athletes find it helps to keep a small notebook with them when they play. During breaks and immediately after the game, they jot down what happened every time they started to feel overly emotional, and after a while they find they don't need to jot things down—that when they start to become upset they can automatically track down the reasons things went wrong.

The Supersensitive tends to see an opponent's verbal and physical aggression as being directed primarily at him. While this could be true if his opponents are baiting him because they know he reacts strongly to such provocation, it may also be that he has misjudged the circumstances and that he is in fact no more the target of such aggressive behavior than is any other member of his team. Sometimes by paying attention to the remarks that may be aimed at other players he will recognize that he is not the target, and thereby become less sensitive to the give and take that accompanies almost any contest.

The Sports Psyching concentration techniques discussed later will be of particular value in helping the overly sensitive player block out such distractions.

4. TENSION CONTROL

This is the ability to cope effectively with your anxiety, to handle pressures and strong feelings in a productive way. If your score is 10 to 25, it means you can usually deal with the anxieties of athletics on a par with most players; that is, it takes a bit to get you rattled.

Low Score (5-10): The Nervous Wreck

The high-strung person often lets his emotions interfere with his performance and ruin his enjoyment. He can slip easily into anxiety before he realizes it. For instance, he might find himself feeling a great deal of pressure over a missed shot and then blow up and miss the next one, and the one after that, growing more tense with each flub. He may be a perfectly rational individual who gets along well with others and acts calmly at home and at work, but on the golf course he may break records for throwing a 5-iron while shouting obscenities.

Typical Comments. "Can't seem to get loose today." "All those people watching make me nervous." "What if I screw up?" "Nothing seems to settle me down today." "Oh, no, this is awful!" "I can't stand it." "God, I'm feeling shaky." "You guys are really putting on the pressure."

Common Behavior. The problems of the Nervous Wreck frequently manifest themselves in a physical way, so that he may experience nausea, sweaty palms, blurred vision, dry throat, and shaky knees during a game.

He may tend to become overly anxious before the contest, so that he makes more errors in the beginning rather than toward the end of the game. The lack of emotional control may also show up in the form of overt anger. Basically, every game for him is an ordeal, so that even if he is ahead he worries constantly about every good shot by his opponent being a turning point against him.

The nervous athlete tends to increase the number of relaxing rituals he goes through before making a play, in order to relieve tension. For instance, a baseball player may at first knock the dirt off his shoes before he comes to bat, but as he begins to get hits and feels a greater pressure to continue his success, he may extend the pre-batting ritual by adjusting his hat, hitching up his pants, and so on—not only to decrease anxiety but actually to delay facing the task. As the anxiety grows, the little habits no longer suffice to overcome it and they become bigger habits. Extremely anxious players may build these habits into lengthy superstitious rituals, which, when they do not work, leave the player with the sense that even his tension-coping devices are no longer of any use to him.

Handling the Situation. The athlete who has high anxiety difficulties is generally aware of it, but by sharply focusing on the emotions as they happen he can frequently halt the problem at that point. That is, by putting himself at some distance from himself and saying, "Okay, there I go again," he can start work on calming himself. Since anxiety and anger can intensify quickly, it is particularly important to be aware of them the moment they start. The Sports Psyching techniques, to be discussed later, are very helpful with this problem.

High Score (25-30): The Iceberg

Ordinarily a high score on Tension Control is not a problem. But it can be if it means such control is stretched to the point where one's game is devoid of emotion. Such an attitude means that when things go wrong one has a cushion against feeling bad, but the converse is that he loses the joy of success. This can stymie the development of skills since one has less motivation to make the effort to improve and reach his full potential.

Typical Comments. "It never bothers me." "It doesn't matter." "I can take it or leave it." "Let's go on to the next play." "I didn't care about that anyway."

Common Behavior. The overcool athlete rarely takes any chances and will play the same type of game whether he is ahead or behind. He plays the percentages and avoids challenges which, if he took them once in a while, could improve his game.

There is a difference between the athlete who genuinely doesn't care and the one who claims he doesn't but whose behavior clearly indicates he does. For instance, the golfer who says that four-putting the last hole didn't really bother him and then steps up to the next tee with a death grip on his club is not recognizing the real meaning to him of doing well or poorly in sports. But the player who claims that all he wants is a social game but who reruns in his own mind, long after the game is over, his successes and mistakes is simply not acknowledging how important athletic prowess is to him.

Handling the Situation. There is no reason why one should not let go once in a while. Emotions, as we have discussed, are intrinsic to sports and there are better, easier ways of dealing with them than by total inhibition. One can derive a great deal more fun from sports by applying the Sports Psyching techniques (to be described) than by taking the stiff-upper-lip approach.

5. CONFIDENCE

This is a belief in your ability. It is having faith in your talents and accepting challenges that test your limits. It is knowing your strengths, acknowledging weaknesses, and going all out in achieving what you can. It means that there is little second guessing about yourself and a willingness to face any obstacles within the range of your capabilities. If you scored between the 10 and 25 range, you have faith in your ability to some degree and accept challenges that are within your range of talents. You are fairly realistic about your strengths and weaknesses.

Low Score (5-10): Insecure

The dearth of self-confidence can become a self-fulfilling prophecy. Frequently, we don't do well at something because we lack faith in our ability to do it, and lack of success then reinforces our defeatist attitude. Not having faith in their capabilities inhibits people from putting forth their best effort. They frequently keep a little in reserve, just enough for them to feel they might have made it *if*—if they had really put their heart into it.

Many individuals are frightened of the pressures of remaining on top which they will feel if they are successful, and so, by expressing lack of confidence, they protect themselves from success. Such athletes start every game expecting to lose. If they win, they think it's a miracle, or luck, no matter how often it happens.

Typical Comments. "I'm a real klutz when it comes to sports." "I'm uncoordinated." "I'm not as good as you guys." "I hope you aren't expecting much of a game from me." "I'll just play along, since I'm not in the same class as you guys."

Common Behavior. Many insecure athletes do not go in much for practicing because they feel it might exhibit their weaknesses. Similarly, some hesitate to take lessons, because they are afraid the instructor will think they're incompetent, or if they do take lessons, they constantly apologize for making mistakes. Others overdo practice because they think they are so bad they require a lot more than most people. They try all kinds of new equipment and buy different new devices, hoping that will give them the confidence they don't have.

Lack of self-confidence is often exhibited in tennis by the failure to make an effort to go after an opponent's best shots, to concede defeat before an effort has been made. The person who lacks confidence also tends to fail to take advantage of those critical situations in which an extra effort at a particular point in the game might be decisive. Thus, even when he knows that the next play may be crucial to the game, he may be unable to galvanize himself into action. When the situation calls for a player to take a chance, the underconfident player generally acts conservatively.

Handling the Situation. Players with a dearth of self-confidence are especially prone toward avoiding self-evaluation. They feel they already know they are "rotten." One can deal with this by checking out his game in detail, nonjudgmentally. Usually he will find that there are individual things he does well, in the context of the game, no matter what the overall level of performance. Furthermore, the things he does poorly will become less threatening, if they can be narrowed down to manageable units.

The Physical Self-Scouting Survey described in the next chapter is particularly useful here. Let's say you are a tennis player who says, "I can't serve to save my life." The Survey will help you define the problem. Perhaps it is that you are not tossing the ball up high enough to give yourself time for a decent swing. Instead of feeling helpless to serve, you could get to work on the toss, and by so doing, find your serve gradually becoming more effective. This, in turn, would give you something on which to build confidence. The cycle of discouragement would be reversed. Knowing that one can *solve problems* can be a great source of inner security. One can build his self-confidence on his ongoing capability to control his own game rather than on the success or failure of every play or the score at the end.

High Score (25-30): Cocky

Cocky people fall into two categories: (1) those who feel they don't need to work because they are so talented, and (2) those who feel compelled to show bravado to cover an inner lack of confidence. Both are unable to learn from their mistakes. This is a special problem of learning which I will explore further in the chapter on how to get the most out of sports instruction.

The overconfident athlete may feel he should be capable of anything and therefore sometimes underestimates challenges. He may appear cocky to others and some may see him as an easy mark for lopsided bets. He may be prone to taking too many risks, always trying for the long shot. A golfer, for example, may be tempted to take risky shortcuts on dog-leg holes because of a misplaced confidence in his ability to hit 225 yards with a 4-wood over 50-foot pine trees and land on the green. Aging tennis star Bobby Riggs has made an entire career out of being the ultimate cocky player. He sets up matches in which he carries a bucket of water or a suitcase in one hand. (But he often wins, because he usually makes certain he is challenging players whose skills he can handle, even with one arm tied behind his back.)

Typical Comments. "Things come easy for me." "Never took a lesson in my life." "I'll spot you five strokes." "Winter rules; you can improve your lie, but I'll play my shots where they fall." "Nothing to it when you know how."

Common Behavior. Frequently, the cocky athlete will fail to do the necessary warm-up exercise before going out on the field and playing. He may also avoid practice sessions, which he may consider to be dull and unnecessary for somebody with his natural flair.

Another sign of the cocky player is that he may give his opponent not only every reasonable break but unnecessary ones as well, conceding relatively long putts or offering to let his opponent take two serves when the rules don't really call for it. In certain sports, such as tennis, if there is some potential disadvantage such as the sun being in one player's eyes and not in the other's, the cocky player will not only offer to play looking into the sun but will keep that side for the entire game, just to show how good he is.

Often he will allow himself to get fairly far behind at the

beginning of a game because he doesn't feel a need to concentrate, believing he can always save the situation later no matter how much he lags behind his opponent.

Cockiness is a trait generally found in the naturally gifted athlete, the kind of person who picks up a set of golf clubs and immediately starts shooting in the low 80s. I have seen a good deal of the overly confident athlete and his problems in observing players moving from one level of sport to another (high school to college, college to professional). The champion at a lower level is frequently unable to put in the effort that is usually necessary on a higher level of competition because his natural talent was never pressed and, therefore, the need for practice and refining of skills wasn't necessary. This may be one of the reasons that some of the players who were not outstanding in college-level play, and who indeed had to work very hard to become good, exceed the talented college player when both get into the pros.

Handling the Situation. The key to whether or not a high score in this category represents a problem is found by separating realistically based self-confidence from the whistling-in-the-dark variety. Confidence about the things one *can* do produces a total effort. So does confidence about being able to achieve realistic goals and improving one's skills. But if a person feels he must have confidence about *everything*, then it is a problem, since there will be times when he will have no capabilities to back up the feelings. Such overestimation of one's abilities may lead to defeat.

The first thing the cocky player needs to do is locate problem areas; the Physical Self-Scouting Survey in the next chapter may provide a nonjudgmental way to accomplish this. The second thing he must do is stop being sensitive about making errors and learn to see them as an opportunity to improve his game; he may need the objective feedback that an instructor can provide, as I discuss in Chapter 13.

6. PERSONAL ACCOUNTABILITY

This is taking personal responsibility for your actions in a game. It is a willingness to face up to your own lapses and to pay the price of trying to correct them. If you were a centerfielder, for example, and the other team scored a run because you were daydreaming as a fly ball flew by you, then, in the context of this definition, you would feel guilty about this. Whether or not this would lead to a constructive response depends a lot on the amount of responsibility you would feel. Too little and you might do nothing; too much and you might become paralyzed with self-destructive feelings. If you score between 10 and 25, you are apt to deal realistically with the balancing of accountability and guilt

Low Score (5-10): Alibi Ike

Athletes scoring low on Personal Accountability have a tendency to alibi. Their impulse when things go wrong is to rationalize too much, to blame everyone and everything but themselves. As a consequence, they tend to feel events are the responsibility of others; the world is to blame, not them. This attitude may thwart them from attempting to improve their skills. It also may tend to isolate them, especially if they are vocal about laying blame, since the Alibi Ike role won't win any popularity contests.

Alibis do not hide under rocks. One can clearly hear himself articulating them. Much of the time one verbalizes this particular problem so that the alibi not only serves a natural purpose of excusing unsatisfactory performance but also explains it to the other players. The other elements in a game—luck, playing conditions, equipment, etc.—are objectively observable and generally shared by all players. It's embarrassing to say, "I can't hit the ball," but much less embarrassing to admit one has hurt one's wrist or that he has tennis elbow.

Typical Comments. "That wind is really bad today." "Damn racquet never was any good." "I can't seem to get the feel of these clubs." "The ball *would* have to take a bounce his way." "The receivers aren't hanging onto my passes today." "This bum knee is sure hurting my game."

Common Behavior. When such persons lose, they tend to blame teammates, the wind, the sun, track conditions, equipment, anything but themselves. They say their opponents cheated or were lucky, that their new shoes pinched, that the weather was rotten, that the ball wouldn't carry because the air was heavy, that the playing surface was in miserable shape. Any or all of these things may have been true. But they become alibis when one's own contribution to a problem is left out.

Handling the Situation. The Alibi Ike type needs to learn to take stock of his game objectively, to evaluate it analytically rather than blame others or himself. Again, the Physical Self-Scouting Survey in the next chapter will be of value here.

High Score (25-30): "Sports Means Always Having to Say I'm Sorry"

The athlete who scores high on Personal Accountability may have a tendency to be too hard on himself, to become angry or depressed with himself for the smallest error. I remember a college quarterback who had entered the game in the second half to save his team, which was being badly beaten. He had been the starting quarterback, but had been injured. Now, he felt, if his team had any chance, it rested with him. During the final two quarters he completed eleven out of twelve passes and directed his team to within two points of winning what appeared to be a hopeless contest. In the process, he set a school pass-completion record. Despite all of his contributions, he was depressed for days because the team had lost. He felt that somehow he had let them down by not having played in the first half, despite the fact it had been recommended he should not have played *at all.* Thus, the overly guilty athlete fails to draw a line separating what was and what was not in his control and tends to take the blame for everything, ignoring the fact that teammates may have had similar missed opportunities or that environmental factors played a part.

Typical Comments. "If only I had done (such and such), I would have won." "Sorry, my fault." "I let everybody down." "Dummy, can't you get anything right?" (to one's self). "I never learn." "I tried, but the harder I try, the worse I seem to get."

Common Behavior. These athletes feel guilty for everything but success. They leave a losing game stoop-shouldered, thinking about all the things they did wrong, and even have trouble fully enjoying a victory. They tend to feel ashamed if they miss a play, and they frequently apologize to the other players for missing. They may even apologize when they have made an excellent shot. Beginners might have a habit of apologizing to their instructor or to more experienced players every time they miss a shot. Not only does their performance and enjoyment suffer because of the anxieties of being guilt-ridden, but their tendency to be depressed and dwell on the negative may spoil the enjoyment of co-players. Because athletic participation is an unpleasant experience, it deters such athletes from putting in the practice needed to improve skills.

Handling the Situation. The first thing the overly guilty athlete must do is work on staking out what he does and doesn't do successfully in any game. When he starts to feel badly about a play, he should ask himself if what happened was really his responsibility. And whenever something was clearly his own fault, he should then ask himself, "What can I do to correct this next time?" The Physical Self-Scouting Survey in the next chapter can be used to focus on what is wrong and keep it in perspective. The major factor one must keep in mind is not to punish himself for errors made in the past, since obviously there is nothing that can be done about them, but to find out just what the errors are and begin to correct them.

7. SELF-DISCIPLINE

This is the willingness to develop and stick to a personal "game plan." Those who score between 10 and 25 are usually able to appraise what they want to do and how they want to do it, then incorporate some form of game organization into their routine, all the while keeping it flexible enough to be changed but stable enough to reflect their talent. It is an attempt for them to become their own coach—knowing their ability and developing their own system. If in golf, for example, one is poor with his wood shots but good with his irons, he needs to organize his game to take advantage of his strength and work on his weaknesses. In basketball, if one is a good playmaker but a poor shooter, it means organizing his game in order to be of maximum benefit to the team. In strategy it represents patience, the ability to stay with one's "game plan" as long as it is working or abandon it only after it has fully proven itself incorrect.

Low Score (5-10): The Chaotic

An undisciplined athlete will start a game with one strategy and, even if it is working, decide to change in midstream because some other strategy strikes his fancy. He also doesn't practice much, and when he does it is often in a haphazard way. He goes along without thinking much about what he'll do next, then tends to choke when he realizes he will have to come up with a counter-strategy.

Many athletes feel that once they have completed the original learning of the fundamentals they then are firmly set in their repertoire and little further practice is needed. Learning new behavior is hard because it requires more work to learn, since you are substituting new disciplines for old and comfortable ones. If you already have a way of doing something and you wish to replace it with a new way of doing something, it generally requires more work than if you have no way of doing something and you are learning how to do it for the very first time. Because of the new difficulties involved, the person with low discipline tends to give up on the new learning very quickly. He ends up with a bundle of things partly learned and poorly executed.

Typical Comments. "If I'd only stuck to the way I was playing it in the early going, I would have won." "I guess I'm just disorganized." "I don't know what possesses me sometimes." "I just don't *think!*" "It seemed like a good idea at the time." "If I could just stick to something, I know I'd win."

Common Behavior. When the pressure is on, the undisciplined athlete tends to break personal rules, often to his detriment. He might start out to play a conservative game of tennis, for example, always trying to make the return, and letting his error-prone opponent make the mistakes. Then his opponent will get in a series of lucky shots. He will then immediately change his game plan. Often he will get angry at himself for allowing himself to be too easily stampeded into things against his better judgment.

Handling the Situation. One of the easiest problems to remedy is that of lack of self-discipline. In practice it is a matter of devising a schedule and simply not allowing oneself to break it until any new material becomes routine. With repeated practice, the new routine becomes a habit. Before playing a game in which specific strategies may be required, one should think about how he wants to play and avoid the tendency to make things up as he goes along or do things differently from the way he did in practice.

The underachieving athlete needs to press himself to work first on those aspects of his game that he does poorest, otherwise he will probably fail to work on them at all. If he sets a time-limit goal on this activity and, on reaching that, moves to other parts of his game, he will find it is possible to improve even those parts that appear beyond repair. By time-limit goal I mean that you work on something for a given period and then stop, regardless of how well you did it. You tell yourself, "I'll practice this play for 20 minutes, then quit." You don't say, "I'll do it till I get it perfect," which would be a performance-limit goal. By setting a time limit rather than a performance limit, the feeling that "Since I'll never get this right I won't bother at all," is overcome.

High Score (25-30): The Lemming

To put in the necessary time and effort in one's strategy is commendable, but some athletes go overboard. They become obsessed with a single strategy and feel guilty if they change the game plan to any degree. The main danger in staying with a single strategy is the possibility of the sport becoming a tedious duty rather than a source of enjoyment. Frequently, rigidity is a sign of insecurity and adherence to one plan simply represents an attempt to feel more secure.

Typical Comments. "That's not the way to do it." "I've got to get it exactly." "I'll get it right if it takes all week." "I think I have to change position a little bit" (even after a successful play). "Are you sure that's the way it looks in the manual?"

Common Behavior. The overly self-disciplined player will practice a single routine in preference to any change. In a game he may even play as if it were a form of practice and not adapt himself to the moment-by-moment requirements of play. Long after a specific set of reactions or strategies has proven itself ineffective, this player will stick to that way of doing things because that's the way he practiced it.

Handling the Situation. The rigid athlete needs to set limits to practicing the same routine before he starts. The practice schedule needs to be varied so it does not dominate the player, and he needs to determine each time how long he will put in on his work. He should work to gain pleasure from the practice he has done and the progress he has made rather than worrying about the need for intensifying a single routine.

When playing a game, one must be prepared to acknowledge that the best laid plans of the most disciplined coaches and players frequently need to be revised. If he has given himself ample opportunity to follow the strategies he planned and they haven't worked out, he should make small revisions in crucial areas and see if he can change the pattern of play without a major overhaul of his previous strategy. One need not change everything in order to gain a significant variation on the way he is playing his game.

TRAIT INTERACTION

Analyzing the combinations.

Now that you have read the descriptions of high and low scores, you can put several of the characteristics together. Try taking your most extreme scores and see what sort of psychological picture you get of yourself. For example, if you are extremely high on Desire but low on Assertiveness, you'll see that you have a burning desire to be number one, but that you can't assert yourself, that, in fact, you're easily intimidated. If you are also high on Personal Accountability, and low on Assertiveness, you may spend more time punishing yourself because you are not successful than asserting yourself enough to be a success. Or if you are high on Assertiveness but low on Tension Control, you may feel free to assert yourself, but your anger regulates your behavior.

Here are some other one-sentence descriptions of different combinations, to provide you with a start for analyzing your profile:

High Confidence—High Sensitivity. You may feel quite capable of doing something, but can be talked out of it by more outspoken, assertive persons.

High Desire—Low Self-Discipline. This means you have a great desire to be successful but try so many different things you hardly show improvement in any area.

High Desire-Low Tension Control. You are very driven to succeed, but keep folding during critical high-pressure points in a game.

High Assertiveness—High Personal Accountability. You may assert yourself freely and perhaps push others around, but you may feel miserable about it later.

This self-scouting is a process, not an end in itself. Ideally it is an *ongoing* process which will help you stay in touch with the psychological factors in your game. After a while it will become automatic and you will line yourself up psychologically just as you now line up your body for a play. You won't feel you're the victim of mysterious forces that sometimes let you play well and other times throw you off.

The categories are not neat—there is some overlap—and obviously the types of behavior described in these categories are subject to multiple interpretations. I have found, however, that at this level of self-awareness athletes are pretty good at doing their own analysis and can judge why they are doing what they are doing. It would be dangerous, however, to try to apply these statements to anyone else's behavior.

Now that you have some ideas about your emotional profile in athletics, let's proceed to an analysis of your physical profile—the actual moves of your game.

SCOUTING YOUR PHYSICAL GAME: 7
Determining the Physical Conflicts

The key is self-analysis, not self-criticism.

I've talked to many players in many sports who have
been in a slump, and they often have the same problem.
Typical is the professional baseball player I counseled who
had gone into a batting slump, dropping from .270 to .240.
It started, according to his batting coach, because of a slight
hitch he developed in his swing. But rather than looking at
this single flaw, he began to become depressed about his
ability to hit at all. And as he lost confidence in his batting
ability, the slump got worse. This, in turn, affected his
performance when he was playing on defense, even though
he had always been a good man with a glove. Soon he was
completely depressed about himself in general.

Does this sound unusual or pathological? Actually, it
is not. Like the ballplayer, most athletes have a hard
time separating themselves from their performance. They
blur all the parts of their game together, judging the
whole by the weakest part. Most players dislike looking
hard at their own performance, because they find the

experience painful and threatening. And when they *do* look, it is usually in the wrong way. They become destructively self-critical, overly judgmental—thus creating more anxiety for themselves.

After some counseling, the ballplayer realized his emotional chain reaction was in itself the problem. We drew up a program for rebuilding his self-confidence which consisted in working on various aspects of his game piecemeal, starting with what he did best and leading up to what he felt were the toughest problems.

The point of this is that many of the emotional problems we've been discussing tie in with having an unrealistic assessment of one's physical ability to achieve goals in athletics. A lot of recreational athletes (and professionals, too) are secretly ashamed of not being able to perform at a much higher level. Never satisfied, they shoot for the moon and despair of their accomplishments.

The problem is their unreasonable or ill-defined expectations do not provide them a realistic context in which to gain satisfaction from their own achievements. It is very important psychologically to have a clear idea of what to expect of yourself in terms of physical performance. You don't have to scale down your expectations, but you do have to be *realistic,* to be able to measure your performance on *your own* terms rather than against some inappropriate standard. Then, when a play or game goes badly, you can isolate the cause and try to correct it rather than berate yourself for blowing it. And you can distinguish things not in your control—for example, basic limitations such as your age, your size, or the amount of time you have to put into your sport—from what is in your control. That's what the baseball player did. He shifted away from destructive self-criticism and into positive self-analysis. That's the difference between self-criticism and self-scouting.

THE PHYSICAL
SELF-SCOUTING SURVEY

How to determine four possible conflicts that hinder performance.

Before getting into a detailed analysis of your game, you should ask yourself how you honestly feel about your physical abilities. Your responses to some general questions will help you determine if you are at the level of competition that really suits you physically and emotionally. It's great to be playing with people who are better than you, but if losing to them is cause for a lot of grief, then you've got a problem. Or perhaps you are talented enough to meet stiffer competition, but are not doing so because being a winner means more to you than playing at your peak. The following Physical Self-Scouting Survey will help to clarify your attitudes toward your talent and its use. There are no "right" answers. The idea isn't to boost or deflate your ego but to find possible *conflicts* that could cause you psychological problems.

THE PHYSICAL SELF-SCOUTING SURVEY

1. I believe my athletic ability is (indicate one): extremely high_____
above average_____ average_____ below average_____ extremely low_____.

2. I am talented enough to participate at the level of competition I desire. Yes_____ No_____ Uncertain_____

3. I am happy with the level of competition at which I participate. Yes_____ No_____ Uncertain_____

4. I have the physical qualifications needed for my sport in terms of:

size: Yes_____ No_____ Somewhat_____
endurance: Yes_____ No_____ Somewhat_____
quickness: Yes_____ No_____ Somewhat_____
strength: Yes_____ No_____ Somewhat_____

5. I have the physical qualifications for the level of competition in which I wish to participate. Yes_____ No_____ Somewhat_____

   If "no," the qualifications I feel I lack are (list):

   _____

   _____

   _____

   _____

6. My strong abilities and talents are (list):

   _____

   _____

   _____

   _____

7. My weak abilities and talents are (list):

   _____

   _____

   _____

   _____

8. My main reasons for sports participation are (indicate):

   competition_____, sociability_____, challenge of the game _____, relaxation_____, diversion_____, business_____, general health and conditioning_____, weight control_____, physician's orders_____.

9. The things I feel capable of improving in my game are (list):

   _____

   _____

   _____

   _____

10. I am willing or able to spend the time to make these improvements. Yes_____ No_____

The conflicts that are revealed by this survey center on four factors:

    1. Capabilities you can't do anything about: age, size, physical potential, and the like.
    2. Capabilities you *can* do something about: strength and speed (within the limits of your physical potential), proficiency in sport skills, time given to practice.
    3. Motivation: how much you want to develop your game.
    4. Ambition: what your goals are.

As you think over your answers to the survey, you may see which of these, if any, come into conflict. For example, if you are 5'6" and weigh 140, and your greatest ambition is to out-drive the top golfer at your club, you obviously have a problem. The same is true if you are overweight, a bit slow, and want to win a trophy in a hot racquet-ball league. Of course, you could go on a diet and do wind sprints to improve speed and stamina, but maybe that conflicts with motivation—the game doesn't really mean that much to you and the main reason you participate is for the sociability.

If you have a conflict, it is best to be aware of it. This may seem obvious, but many people just don't want to sit down and think how their talents, capabilities, motivations, and goals in sports actually conflict or fit together. But if there are aspects of your physical game that bother you now, the best way to resolve such conflicts is to single out the things you want to change and determine if there is something you realistically can do about them. If you like skiing but are hampered by lack of strength in your legs, you could work out at a gym for a couple of months to strengthen them. If you don't *feel* like doing this, then you should admit to yourself that you are willing to live with

your limitations—and not eat your heart out at your failure
to be the downhill racer you'd like to be.

TWO RULES FOR PHYSICALLY
SCOUTING YOURSELF

Keep it analytical, keep it constructive.

Now that you've sorted out the larger conflicts that
impede your game, here are two rules for analyzing them
further.

✱ Rule 1: Divide and Conquer

Go from the general to the specific. By isolating problems, you can keep emotional brush fires under control.
Then you won't have a problem in one part of your game
affecting the other parts, as happened with the baseball
player I mentioned, who let anxiety about his batting slump
affect his fielding and his abilities in general. In working
with him, we found isolating his problems made them
manageable again.

Breaking problems down into parts makes them less
threatening and more accessible to solution. This is because
it gives you something specific to deal with. It puts things
into perspective. The problem is now seen for what it is—a
part of your performance rather than all of it.

Break your game into its natural segments, its basic
functional units. All sports have distinct parts. With tennis,
for example, you can check out the various kinds of
strokes: forehand, backhand, serve, overhead, lobs, ground
strokes, and so on. Each swing of the racquet also can be
divided into segments: stance, grip, position to approach

ball, backswing, impact, follow-through, recovery. Team sports can be broken down into the specific tasks of the position one plays: the blocks, tackles, and plays a lineman in football makes; the dribbling, passing, rebounding, assists, field goals, and free throws required of a basketball forward. If you are uncertain about the exact components of a particular move, see a physical instruction book or ask an instructor or coach.

List the tasks of your game and rank them. Start with those you do best and proceed to those you do with least success. Remember, this ranking should be *relative to your own game,* not measured against absolutes or outside factors. If as a tennis player you feel your serve is the most reliable part of your game, rank it number one, regardless of whether or not your serve is very good. Rate your performance of each basic functional unit on a percentage scale.

The scale you use should be based on how often you reach your top potential on that particular segment. If, for example, you consider a good golf drive for you to be 195 yards, then rate the percentage of times you are able to hit the ball 195 yards or more on a typical day. Allow yourself 100 percent only for those parts of your game that typically match your *top* performance—the peak efforts of the best game you recall ever playing (unless, of course, you're a fifty-year-old trying to duplicate those days when you were captain of your college tennis team). All players have periods when their performances are better than usual, when they are "on" their game. This should be your point of reference.

You might break down your golf game as to how often you hit your best shot in each category. For example:

Chips—hit best shot 80 percent of the time,
Putts—best shot 75 percent of the time,
Short irons—60 percent,

Fairway woods—50 percent,
Drive—50 percent,
Long irons—30 percent.

The next time you practice, you could use this information to concentrate on what most needs work—in this case, your long irons. After you have worked on improving your long iron shots, you will have a precise way of measuring progress, by checking to see if the percentage for that category has risen.

Initially, this self-examination may make you feel self-conscious about your game. But this is an advantage because you now are becoming aware of specific causes of problems. Rather than worrying about final scores and being pre-occupied with poor results (the ends), you will now be shifting your focus to the process by which the poor results came about (the means).

Rule 2: Deal with Problems Analytically, Not Judgmentally

Say, "My long iron shots need some work," not "I'm lousy with long irons." From there analyze and isolate more. "I tend to slice my long iron shots about 40 percent of the time." Zero in *analytically* even more: "My trouble with the long irons is that I tend to let my right elbow fly when I swing. I also tend to be intimidated when I have to use my long irons. I believe that one of the reasons I let the elbow fly is to overcompensate for my nervousness about getting the ball off. I try to muscle the ball too much, and so I put too much right-arm power into the down-swing too soon; that causes the flying elbow, which then causes the slice."

With this analysis it is relatively easy to pinpoint actions to take to start rectifying the problem. You can say to yourself, "I'll remember to keep that elbow close to my body on those shots, and I'll feel less nervous, too, because I know exactly the source of the problem and because I am doing something about it."

Try to keep this nonjudgmental approach uppermost in mind. If you are a skier, for example, you can learn exactly when to shift your weight to make a difficult turn and at the same time reduce any fear of falling. You can say to yourself, "I'll begin to shift my weight just at this part of the hill and in that way I'll be prepared to slow down. It will also reduce my fear of falling." Remember, when you find out what you are doing wrong, it is a step *forward*, not something to be ashamed of. You have succeeded in *identifying* the problems—and until you do that, the Sports Psyching techniques I'm going to talk about in the following chapters won't be as helpful.

Sometimes being nonjudgmental won't be enough. Whenever you reach a point where you have broken down your game, have been as analytical as you can, but *still* aren't clear on what's causing a problem, it's a good idea to consult an instructor. What is happening (and does happen often, with pros as well as with amateur players) is that you cannot always observe yourself completely—either physically, because you can't see the moves, or emotionally, because you don't want to admit something to yourself. It is important to realize there are some problems that only a trained person watching you can detect; so it is better to spend a few dollars for a brush-up lesson rather than sink into despair. Seeking help is the most natural thing in the world. The professional teams constantly work at this, with coaches for every position or skill. And the very best individual-sport players also do it all of the time. (If you watched Jimmy Connor's big matches, you would have seen his coach Pancho Segura on the sidelines counseling him almost every time there was a change of sides.) The point is that there's no reason why you should not make occasional lessons a regular part of your sports activities.

SELF-SCOUTING AS AN ONGOING PROCESS

Stop making the same mistakes over and over.

Self-scouting should be just what the term implies—done by you and for you. The Sports Emotional-Response Profile and the Physical Self-Scouting Survey were meant only to prime the pump from which you now should be able to draw useful information anytime you play.

You have some ideas now about how psychological and physical factors work in your game. Now it's time to see how this happens in actual play. This will help you move even further from the more general concepts we have been discussing to first-hand personal experience. This doesn't mean some ponderous self-analysis. Just make a mental note to observe yourself the next few times you go out for a game. This is the first time you take these lessons into the field. The purpose is not to change your game—yet—but to see how much more accurate you can make your scouting reports.

Look at your behavior both from physical and psychological standpoints. See how accurate your Self-Scouting Survey was and make any changes in it you think valid. At the same time, notice what happens to you emotionally and check how this fits in with your SERP results. Now put the two aspects together. How did the physical and psychological factors work together? What was your frame of mind as you made exceptionally good plays? How often did less than satisfactory plays coincide with psychological problems—anxieties, anger at another player, distractions? Make a mental note of what started you off each time you became emotional.

Perhaps, you may feel, some of the information you have just obtained was familiar to you all along, and the problem, you may say, is not just knowing what's wrong but being able to do something about it. If that's what you are thinking now, you are ready for the next chapters; you are ready to go from self-knowledge to self-improvement.

SPORTS PSYCHING:
Learning to Repeat
the Best Day You Ever Had

Psyching yourself fully into your game.

Whether beginner or pro, each of us can recall positive moments when everything seemed to click. Think over the times when you've made your greatest plays. Probably the major element that you'll recall will be that, at the time, you were *totally involved* in what you were doing, unconscious of yourself as the doer, aware only of the done. Indeed, the time of that extraordinary performance usually lasts only as long as you are not self-consciously aware of it. When you said, "Aren't I doing fantastically?" the fantasy evaporated.

These high moments have four qualities in common:

1. You are physically free. Your body is able to move naturally, seemingly on its own, unhampered by tensions. You may at the time even have been surprised at your own strength, speed, or agility, even though there was no strain.

2. You are mentally focused. Your attention is directed to the action, to the here and now. You are concerned only with the activity of making the play and not thinking about past or future.

3. You are in harmony. No part of you conflicts with another. Mind and body work together. You are moving with the action and have the feeling of being one with it.

4. You are enjoying it. The experience is pleasurable, not just in terms of satisfaction with the results—it simply feels right. Athletes who are really involved frequently describe a play in terms of its beauty. They are even able to feel joy in an opponent's play when the execution has that special quality.

These magic moments do not derive from mysterious forces: they are the product of certain psychological conditions—and we can make *them* happen more and more frequently. Let's talk about how to to that, for that, in fact, is what this entire book is about.

THE PREPARATION/PRACTICE/ PLAY APPROACH

Getting into the state of mind and body that allows you the best chance at peak performance.

Most players think they can't do much about whether or not they are "on" their game. When you're hot, you're hot; when you're not, you're not, they figure.

But you don't *have* to wait for it to happen; you really can do something about it. Although you can't be hot 100 percent of the time, you can play at your best consistently— much more often than you probably are now. You can do so by learning a deliberate, conscious method that supplies a set of psychological tools you can call upon in your game. You can do this with a three-step routine I've called the Preparation/Practice/Play Approach, which is described in detail in the next three chapters. Here's how it works.

Preparation: Relaxed Concentration

In this stage, you put yourself into the state of mind and body most conducive to achieving your best in athletics. Because you play best when your body is loose and limber, in this Preparation stage you learn how to physically *relax* more easily, more deeply, so that you'll be able to relax yourself at will when you start becoming too keyed up during a game. And because you also play your best when your mind is clear and focused on the action, in this first stage you learn techniques to *concentrate* more readily, so that you can shut out distractions.

This state of *relaxed concentration* is not some sort of exotic trance—nothing you've never done before—but a way of keeping anxiety from getting the upper hand so you can better channel the energy of the game's excitement into productive performance. You may still become anxious during competition, of course, but at least now the emotions that are always a part of sports will add to the excitement of your game rather than destroy it.

Practice: Overlearning the Techniques

The moves in sports are often complicated, and it is easy to forget details and to slip into mistakes. No matter how relaxed you are and how well you are concentrating, if you move the wrong way or if your swing or other skill technique is faulty, the play will be unsuccessful. Moreover, if you are always consciously *thinking* about how you will make a play—how, for example, you will hold your racquet and what foot you will lead off with as the serve comes at you over the net—these very thoughts will become a distraction. There is a difference between relaxed concentration that facilitates skillful play by reducing distractions and self-consciousness about your skills that is itself a distraction. For this reason, skills should be overlearned. As when you're driving a car, your actions have to be so well learned that they are automatic.

The techniques in the Practice stage will help you learn faster and more effectively and will help you remember the skills to use when you need them. And not only will they sharpen your physical skills, they will also improve your game from a psychological standpoint. From the SERP and Physical Self-Scouting Survey you should now know what your faulty habits are, but it's almost impossible to break these habits unless you have new ones to replace them. If you automatically react in a way you don't like—for example, you become intimidated too easily when you fall behind in a game when you should be redoubling your concentration and reassessing your strategy—you can use the techniques of this Practice stage to build more productive kinds of behavior into habits that will automatically replace the problem reactions you've identified.

Play: Using Sports Psyching

In this stage you will be able to employ the Sports Psyching techniques of the Preparation and Practice stages so that, in just a few seconds, you can let go and commit yourself fully to the action of the game. Gradually building up your positive experiences to reinforce confidence, you will accustom yourself to using Sports Psyching techniques in actual competition. Almost every player has a ritual or device or "good luck charm" that he believes relieves the tensions of athletics. For example, he may yank at his hat, shuffle his feet, or wear only green socks when he plays golf. But now the Sports Psyching techniques will be a ritual part of your game—but a lot more effective than green socks. Once you learn your Sports Psyching routine, you can use it as a brief, productive, private ritual before a game and before the start of each game segment, to control pressure, focus your energies, and get yourself set for your best chance at a successful play.

SIX WEEKS TO A BETTER GAME

A program to strengthen your ability to deal with the emotional side of your game.

The Sports Psyching techniques take time to learn. I have set out a plan of six weeks from the time you start to learn the techniques until you are able to employ them in actual play. For all of us, impatient for improvement, six weeks may seem like a very long period indeed. When you consider, however, how long it took you to acquire the habits you are trying to change and how deeply imbedded they are, the six-week period won't seem quite so long. And at the end of that time you will be playing with an awareness and a relaxed concentration which previously you enjoyed only on your very best days.

It is as important that you not jump ahead of yourself in working on these techniques as it would be for you if you were learning a physical aspect of a sport. Trying harder won't shorten the time and should be avoided. The program is broken down into manageable steps, each of which leads to the next. If you have problems with one step, go back a step until you feel comfortable at that level, then continue.

The amount of time needed to learn these techniques is small—up to 20 minutes a day for six weeks. That is a total of 12½ hours over more than a month's time—not much, considering what you will be gaining.

→ The six-week program is as follows:

The first two weeks will be for learning *relaxation* techniques—"Getting Loose" and "Breathing Easy." The third week you'll learn *concentration*—"Staying on the Ball." This will complete the Preparation stage.

The fourth and fifth weeks, still continuing with relaxation and concentration techniques, you will add *Mental Rehearsal*, in which you mentally rehearse the successful moves of your game. The sixth week you'll add *Body Rehearsal*, in which you physically rehearse the correct moves. This completes the Practice stage.

After that you can put the techniques of Preparation and Practice into Play. You will employ the relaxation, concentration, Mental Rehearsal, and Body Rehearsal techniques as a brief warm-up routine and in other ways that will help you play your best game.

WHY SPORTS PSYCHING WORKS

The body-mind division is arbitrary.

The Sports Psyching techniques can be used for any sport, whether individual or team. I will give examples for only some sports, but the principles apply across the board and you will be able to fit them into your particular sport at the level of competition you play. Moreover, once you learn to use them in one sport you can readily apply them to another. This is because, just as the pressures I discussed earlier occur in all sports, the remedies are effective in all sports.

The techniques can be used to deal with specific problems, whether psychological or physical. The reason is, as I have emphasized throughout this book, that the division between the mental and physical is arbitrary. They are two ways of looking at the same, unified experience and we separate them in order to be able to better analyze and understand it. Since physical performance and psychological problems go hand in hand, the Sports Psyching techniques are a combined physical-psychological approach.

You start with the body—by relaxing it—and this also clears emotional distractions from the mind. In the next step, you focus the mind with concentration exercises—and this also helps keep your body relaxed. From the relaxed concentration of the Preparation stage you go to Practice, with Mental Rehearsal of the actions you will need to perform. While this is an exercise of the mind—reinforcing the memory responses you'll need while you play—it also sets up the proper physical responses for your muscles to follow; it helps "groove" the correct performance. The Body Rehearsal technique is the most overtly physical of the four. It is a sort of shadow-boxing procedure by which you make sure you get the physical feeling for the right moves, but it also has psychological results, in that it fixes the sensations of correctly executed play more firmly in your memory. The Body Rehearsal also reinforces your confidence in carrying out the play successfully, thus minimizing anxieties about errors.

Thus, the Preparation and Practice stages are combinations of mind-body exercises, so that when you go into the Play stage you can continue in the same step-by-step manner, thus being able to commit yourself to the action without the inhibitions caused by anxieties.

You start out at home or some place where you can be alone and eventually learn to feel comfortable with the techniques in a practice situation and then finally in competition. This successive method of learning is a psychologically sound way of gaining a thorough knowledge of each technique, along with building confidence in using it.

GETTING THE MOST OUT OF SPORTS PSYCHING

You can't just read a book about it.

You may feel that just reading the book is enough, that there is no need for you to actually practice any of this stuff. And you may indeed be able to utilize the Sports Psyching techniques (particularly the relaxation techniques) in some way without any practice to improve your game. But it's unlikely that the improvement will last very long if this is all that you do. Slowly, the relaxed concentration and awareness will drift away and you will fall back on older, stronger habit patterns. It happens all the time and you are not exempt from what we psychologists know of the laws of learning. If, however, you want to benefit from these techniques—not next weekend but a year from next weekend, and ten years from next weekend—you will undertake the program as it is described in the following pages.

A commonly known phenomenon in psychology is the *placebo effect*. It means that if you are convinced something will happen, you will unconsciously *make* it happen. This effect occurs in about 30 percent of cases, whether or not the individual follows instructions properly to reach the program's promised goal. In other words, if none of the readers of this book did anything but just read the techniques, three out of ten of them would still show improvement at their sport—just because they believed in it and tried something different. But—and this is most important—the improvement wouldn't last. It is not my purpose in writing this book to produce just a temporary placebo effect. Do the exercises; and do them on a regular basis.

Use the techniques to achieve realistic goals. If you are a Sunday golfer, for example, you might be able to shave five or even ten strokes off your score over a period of time, but don't expect to end up playing like Jack Nicklaus. Don't make a contest out of all this or try to rush it. If you put pressure on yourself to perform the techniques themselves or substitute the worry about how well you're playing with the worry about how well you're relaxing or concentrating, then you'll be defeating the whole purpose of Sports Psyching. Learn the techniques in the way that feels most comfortable to you. I've set out six weeks as a generally optimum time, but don't consider this a deadline. Go at your own pace.

No doubt a question in your mind is, "Can I use the Sports Psyching right away in play or do I have to wait the full six weeks?" The answer is: of course you can start using it right away--during the first week of the program, in fact, if you like. What you want to avoid, however, is trying to rush the program. In the first week when you start the Sports Psyching exercises, they will immediately have some effect—not a great effect, just some effect. However, if you expect spectacular improvement right off, you'll be disappointed. Don't keep taking your temperature, judging the results of the program by the result of a single day's activity. Concentrate on learning the techniques first and don't worry about results until you have the techniques down pat. After that the improvements in your game will come on their own. A word of caution: Don't talk about the program with your co-players. It will make you feel that you then have to prove how good it is by showing them what an improved player you've become. If they ask you about it, you can certainly tell them what you are doing, but if you volunteer this information, you will end up adding another extraneous pressure to your game.

While you may feel a bit self-conscious about using the Sports Psyching techniques at first, remember they don't require you to do anything outwardly unusual during the game itself. If you find yourself not accustomed to taking deliberate steps to relax yourself, concentrate, and so on, recall how it was when you first learned the physical skills of your game—remember how the first motions seemed awkward and that it took a while before you were able to handle the equipment and make the required moves with some ease. The learning process for Sports Psyching is similar.

If you feel uncomfortable at any step, don't go ahead. Simply back up to the previous step. Expect that your improvement will progress, but not on a uniformly rising curve. There will be some occasions when it will level off temporarily or even dip. When learning any skill, we tend to go in spurts. Don't become discouraged if this happens.

Now let's get to it.

PREPARATION: 9
Getting Loose, Breathing Easy, and Staying on the Ball

Putting yourself into the state of mind and body to play relaxed and concentrated.

The advice to the aspiring athlete used to be: Exercise, eat nutritious foods, get plenty of rest. To that we've now added: Learn a relaxation technique.

Pitchers tug at their caps before the throw. Golfers waggle their clubs after teeing up. Basketball players breathe deeply before making the free throw. Just about all athletes, in fact, have some ritual to relax themselves, to relieve tension.

The Oakland Raiders' George Blanda, all-time National Football League scorer, says that when he's called upon to kick a long-yardage, clutch field goal "the main thing is to try to relax, to stay loose. If I start tensing up or try to muscle the ball, I'll be off." Relaxation is necessary, then, to break the emotional snowballing effect caused by negative emotions such as anxiety and anger, which divert your play. Indeed, relaxing your body not only stops the snowballing, it reverses it: as your body relaxes, it has a calming effect on your mind, and anxieties subside.

This principle of body-mind interaction has been long established. In 1920, Edmund Jacobson, Chicago physician and physiologist, showed that one simply *cannot* experience anxiety when muscle tension is reduced. The author of many books on relaxation *(Progressive Relaxation, Tension in Medicine, The Biology of Emotions)*, Jacobson demonstrated that if the physiological manifestations of an emotion were removed, so was the emotion itself. In other words, you can't be on opposite ends of the physiological-emotional spectrum at the same time—if your body is calm, for instance, you can't be edgy. Thus, Jacobson found, getting the tension out of your muscles also diminishes the anxiety that caused it.

But he also found that when you're keyed up, your muscles won't relax with just a verbal command. Telling yourself, "Relax, Charlie" won't work; when you're emotional, your muscles are more tense than you realize.

You can, however, *teach* yourself to relax tense muscles. Jacobson put his patients through a series of exercises in which they first flexed their muscles from head to foot, then held them at a high level of tension, and then quickly let go. This demonstrated that deliberately holding a muscle at a high level of tension until it tired, then releasing the tension, made the muscle relax much more than it would ordinarily. You can prove this to yourself: Sit in a chair, hold one leg straight out in front of you for as long as you can, then let it drop. Your leg muscles will automatically go into a very relaxed state, to compensate for the hard work they just finished. Jacobson found that when his patients had done these exercises for a while, they could make a muscle relax simply by giving it the command to do so—without first performing the exercises. In doing the tension-release exercises, they had *learned* how to let go fully whenever they wished.

This relaxation effect also can be produced by drugs.

Alcohol in moderate quantities has some relaxing effect. So does marijuana. Certain tranquilizers not only work on the nervous system, but reduce the level of tension in the muscles, which contributes to the lowering of emotions. But, obviously, you don't want to drug yourself in order to relax during an athletic contest. Besides, there are better, more natural methods of relaxing.

Dr. Herbert Benson, associate professor of medicine at Harvard Medical School and director of the hypertension section at Boston's Beth Israel Hospital, describes one such method in his best-selling 1975 book, *The Relaxation Response*. Benson taught hundreds of patients a meditation technique which they practiced every day. Similar to Transcendental Meditation and the meditative practices found in nearly all religions, the method consists of repeating a simple sound, word, or phrase (called a mantra in Sanskrit) such as the word "One." Benson's patients would retire to a quiet, private room, make themselves comfortable, and then repeat the word "One" quietly to themselves for 20 minutes. With continued daily practice, the method produced not only a very relaxed feeling but also positive health results, including even lowering of the blood pressure for some people.

Benson's method is the opposite of Jacobson's in that it works from the mental to the physical. By putting the mind's attention on the mantra, and keeping it free of disturbing thoughts, the *body* automatically relaxes itself. But whatever relaxation method one practices—Jacobson's, Benson's, Transcendental Meditation, self-hypnosis, or yoga-style breathing exercises—if you do it for 20 to 60 minutes a day it will definitely improve your well-being. Depending on the method, the state of relaxation can be dreamy and slightly euphoric, akin to floating, or it can be a spiritual-mystical experience, as occurs in certain religious meditation.

All of us need a period each day when we can relax and recharge ourselves. It has been demonstrated that such relaxation sessions can reduce the body's lactic acid (which builds up with fatigue) as much as would eight hours of sleep, and that after a period of time some people show better circulation and a reduction of many of the health problems associated with stress. And, to get back to sports, doing a half-hour relaxation session once a day will help your game, just like regular exercise, good nutrition, or anything that makes you feel better.

However, we are most concerned with relaxation techniques that will help you loosen up *just before and during a game*. On the court or field you need some way to quickly and effectively reverse the emotional snowballing effect when anxieties strike, and obviously you can't go off and put yourself into a deep meditation or relaxation state. You need an unobtrusive, nondisruptive way to level off when the pressures start to put you into a nosedive. Through your self-scouting, you are aware of the kinds of sports situations which are most likely to generate negative emotions in you. Now let us start learning the Sports Psyching techniques so you can condition yourself to relax on cue and begin to cope with those situations.

The two relaxation techniques are "Getting Loose" and "Breathing Easy." We will show you how to learn these techniques by yourself in a nonthreatening situation. You will learn to associate the calming sensations with a cue word, so that at the end of the six-week program you will be able to cue yourself into relaxation before or during a game. The cue for "Getting Loose" will be: *"Let go."* The cue for "Breathing Easy" will be: *"Easy."*

Now, let's see what you need to do the first week— starting today.

THE FIRST WEEK: SPORTS PSYCHING TECHNIQUE NO. 1– "GETTING LOOSE"

Whether a play calls for power or finesse, you need to be loose.

What "Getting Loose" Is

Watch any game and during breaks you'll likely see athletes doing things like letting their arms dangle, shaking their hands at their sides, rolling their shoulders, stretching and bending down, letting their heads and necks roll about, running in place, doing little dances on the sidelines. They are, of course, trying to "get loose," to work out the tension that builds up in their muscles.

Sports isn't all muscle power by any means; skill is the telling factor. Even weightlifting, which you might assume was pure power, demands precise timing and coordination. The skilled moves required in all sports demand that you flex *and relax* muscles in a certain sequence. In archery, for example, the release of the bowstring is everything; you have to be able to do it smoothly, without "plucking the harp." In a golf swing, you have to release the power you put into the downswing by going with the centrifugal force of the club head at just the right moment. In other words, it is the fluidity in a movement that counts—the combination of tightening for muscle power and then letting go as arms, shoulders, back, and legs go through a swing or a kick or a throw.

What "Getting Loose" Does

Whether a play calls for power or finesse, you need to be loose. When Jack Nicklaus knows he needs an extra long tee shot he says, "My objective is to get good and relaxed." Slammin' Sammy Snead's advice for drives or pressure putts is the same: "Get loose as a goose." This looseness doesn't mean go limp. It means free yourself from unnecessary muscle tension.

Anxiety makes the release part of any physical move more difficult. You can feel the discomfort of knotted muscles. Your muscles tend to stay tense; they won't let go. With most people, tension is felt in one part of the body more than others. It hits some in the neck, others in the back, others in the legs. Part of this may be fatigue from the sport itself, of course, but it is exacerbated by anxiety.

The "Getting Loose" technique, which works on Jacobson's tension-release principle, functions as a feedback device. That is, in learning the technique you heighten your awareness of muscle tension itself and become more alert to residual tension in your body. You will be in a better position to tell when anxieties are creeping up on you because you'll more quickly recognize the feeling of muscles beginning to knot up—especially in whatever area of your body this tends to be most pronounced. Once you recognize the tension, you will have the means to do something about it. You will be able to cue your muscles to "let go" and they will loosen up. Your own tension will be an automatic reminder for you to relax before each play.

How to Learn "Getting Loose"

Allot yourself a 10-minute period each day for the next seven days to work on this. Pick a time that is comfortable for you and a place where you can be in private and won't be disturbed; a bedroom is best. Just before going to bed at night is convenient for most people; it will help you get to sleep. (This can also be a drawback, for if you are fatigued you are liable to drop off before you've had time to work on learning the technique.) Right after you get home from work is another good time, since this is relaxation, after all. It's probably best, however, not to do it directly after dinner. You may well want to do this more than once a day, too. Whatever time you pick, try to make it the *same* time every day. This will help you stick to your daily routine; moving the time around makes it too easy to keep postponing it. Actually, you'll find this a pleasant experience, and you may want to schedule it to give you a refreshing break in your day.

Begin each 10-minute session as follows:
Loosen your clothing and remove your shoes.

Lie down with a pillow under your head (on a bed or on the floor).

Lie flat on your back, feet about 12 to 18 inches apart, arms at your sides.

Go as limp as you can from head to foot.

Let your shoulder blades go slightly flat.

Wag your feet; settle in with your legs.

Shake your arms gently, rolling the backs of your hands against the floor.

Roll your head back and forth.

Now begin the "Getting Loose" exercise for each part of your body, as follows:

1. **Left leg.** Flex the muscles of your left leg by raising it 6 to 10 inches above the floor. Point your toes slightly back toward your head.

Hold this position of tension for as long as you can, about 10 seconds or so, until you begin to feel the muscles start to tremble.

Then, say to yourself, *Leg, let go.*

At this point, *stop* flexing it and *let* the leg drop.

Let the leg rest for another 10 seconds or so, saying to yourself: *I feel the tension flowing out of my leg. . . . My leg feels relaxed, warm, heavy . . . completely relaxed. . . .*

Repeat the flex-let go-rest procedure for that leg.

2. Right leg. Run through the entire procedure twice for your right leg.

3. Buttocks and thighs. Tighten your buttock and thigh muscles, as tightly as you can.

Hold them as long as you can—longer than 10 seconds—until you *have to* let go.

Then release them, saying, *Let go,* to yourself.

Pause for 10 seconds or so and focus your attention on the relaxed feeling in those muscles, on the tension flowing out.

Repeat the exercise.

4. Stomach. Do the same procedure twice for your abdominal muscles.

5. Back and neck. Arch your spine, tightening all along it from your tailbone to your neck, and finish by telling it, *Let go.*

Repeat the exercise.

6. Arms and shoulders. Imagine there is a bar suspended above you that you want to use to pull yourself up.

Raise your hands, palms upward, above your chest.

Grab the imaginary bar and clench your fists around it as hard as you can.

Flex the muscles in your arms and shoulders.

Hunch your shoulders up as tightly as you can.

Hold as long as possible, then say, *Let go.*

Rest for 10 seconds or so, soaking up the warm, relaxed feelings, letting the tension flow out.

Repeat the exercise.

7. Jaw. Tighten your jaw muscles, clamping down on your back teeth.

Say, *Let go*, and relax.

Repeat the exercise.

8. Face. Tighten your facial muscles into a strong grimace.

Say, *Let go*.

Rest and focus on the relaxing feeling.

Repeat the exercise.

9. Eyes. Focus on a point on the ceiling.

Then, not moving your head, slowly roll your eyes to the right as far as they will go, then to the center, then to the left, then back to the center.

Repeat.

Rub the palms of your hands together until you feel heat.

Close your eyes and cover them with your hands.

Let the heat warm them.

Rest, and tell your eyes, *Let go*, and feel the tension flow out as you feel the warmth.

10. Entire body. Clench your feet and fists. Pull your shoulders up. Tighten your jaw and face.

Now simultaneously flex your entire body, arching yourself as much as you can from your heels to the back of your head. Hold it for as long as you can, until you feel your body tremble.

Then say, *Let go*—and just let yourself go . . . all the way, as much as you can.

Lie there and feel the tension drain away.

11. Get totally relaxed. Close your eyes. Let your attention wander slowly over each part of your body, from legs to face, as you did in the exercise. If any area seems to have some residual tension, tell it, *Let go.*

Feel the tension draining out of you, but don't worry if there is still a little left.

Keeping your eyes closed, stay in this relaxed state for the rest of the 10-minute session.

Think of a very pleasant, peaceful place. Think of floating in a small boat on a peaceful lake with a soft breeze gently rocking you back and forth, back and forth. Or think of floating in space, lighter than air, weightless.

Observe the pleasant, calm feelings.

Tell yourself: *I am relaxed now. . . . My legs feel relaxed. . . . My buttocks, thighs, and abdomen feel relaxed. . . . My back, arms, shoulders, jaws, face, and eyes feel relaxed. . . . The tension has been let go.*

12. Focus your relaxed feelings. Now begin to focus this relaxation on your game.

Tell yourself: *When I am playing and I begin to feel tension gripping some muscles, I will be able to tell those muscles, "Let go." Saying, "Let go", will recall the relaxed feelings I feel now and will release the tension from those muscles.*

That's the "Getting Loose" Sports Psyching exercise. As I said, you should perform it every day at the same time in the same place for 10 minutes. Note that throughout the technique "letting go" is not something you *do;* you don't *make* your leg drop. It's like the difference between throwing a ball and letting it drop out of your hand. The point is to learn to *let* tension go out of your muscles and to associate this release with the cue phrase, "Let go."

In addition, don't worry about how deeply relaxed the muscles get. As you follow this routine throughout the second week, the relaxation effect will improve until it reaches its fullest.

Do the "Getting Loose" exercise for a week. You will then be ready for "Breathing Easy."

THE SECOND WEEK: SPORTS PSYCHING TECHNIQUE NO. 2– "BREATHING EASY"

Learning to do what comes naturally—breathing easy.

What "Breathing Easy" Is

"One way to break up any kind of tension is good deep breathing," said golfer Byron Nelson. Many top athletes (among them Johnny Miller and Rod Laver) use breathing exercises to relieve anxieties, and breathing techniques have been used by modern Western psychotherapists as well as ancient yoga teachers. We are all familiar with the fact that when we're anxious, we sigh or otherwise blow out air to let off the tension. Taking deep breaths and slowing down the breathing rate is not only a natural and effective way to calm yourself, it also counters one of the more troublesome physical symptoms of anxieties: rapid, shallow breathing.

What "Breathing Easy" Does

You breathe some 20,000 times a day, or about fourteen times per minute, tensing and relaxing certain muscles each time. When you inhale, you use the muscles of your diaphragm and chest to expand your rib cage, which is constructed like a sort of spring device, and your lungs, which are made of elastic tissue. This creates a partial vacuum, resulting in air rushing into your nose or mouth, down your windpipe into the bronchial tubes, and finally into the lungs themselves. When you exhale, you relax, you let go. You release those diaphragm muscles, and your rib cage and lungs naturally contract, causing air to flow outward. What you are doing is inhaling and letting go, inhaling and letting go.

Nervousness, however, tends to constrict the muscles in your diaphragm, chest, and throat so they don't let go as much. Thus, you begin to breathe more shallowly and—to make up for less air going in and out during each breath—more rapidly. If you are exerting yourself at the same time, as in sports, this compounds the problem: you need more air and at the same time your breathing is being inhibited by tension.

It is no coincidence that the term for being overwhelmed by emotional pressure in sports is "to choke"—you are literally choking yourself. This condition, in turn, adds to anxiety. It stimulates feelings of being out of control. After all, the quickest way to panic is to have your air cut off. Minimal interference with your breathing is enough to be very threatening at an unconscious level. Whereas fright, horror, and anxiety may be said to "take your breath away," the expression, "you can breathe easy," describes the opposite reaction. Release from tension means freedom to breathe. You are back in control; the world no longer closes in on you.

Biologically, rapid breathing makes you take in a lot of oxygen and expel most of your carbon dioxide, preparing you for immediate violent action. The trouble is, your body tends to go overboard and can get rid of so much CO_2 that it upsets the carbon dioxide-oxygen balance in your blood stream. This effect is called hyperventilation, and if it goes on long enough, certain nerve centers respond by shutting things down momentarily in defense to force you to resume breathing normally. In other words, you faint. Hyperventilation, however, is extreme. What nearly always happens is that the crisis passes, the tension peaks and subsides, and your breathing slows down and deepens.

Generally, your body gets its roller-coaster ride as you react unconsciously to various stimuli, and if such stimuli are commonly generated in the course of a game, your level of performance is bound to deteriorate. That is, you are not in very good control. You can regain that control, however, by bringing up to a conscious level your ability to release tension through "breathing easy." Deliberately slowing and deepening your breathing for a short while will have a calming effect, for by reasserting your control over a most vital function—breathing—it will give you a sense of assurance. It will redirect your attention from anxiety-causing distractions and focus it upon your own breathing and upon the fact that you are reasserting control over yourself.

How to Learn "Breathing Easy"

In this second week, you should extend your daily exercise to 20 minutes. Start with the "Getting Loose" exercise as before and practice that for 10 minutes. Then spend a minute breathing normally.

Now, still lying on your back, do the "Breathing Easy" exercise, for 10 minutes, as follows:

1. **Inhale.** Inhale slowly and deeply, filling your chest with air, counting four seconds to yourself, *One and two and three and four.* . . . The count is to give you a nice and easy, even pace.

Try to breathe as fully as you can without discomfort. Imagine your chest slowly filling with air, from your diaphragm to your collar.

2. Hold breath. When you have inhaled fully, hold your breath for another four seconds, again counting to yourself, *One and two and* . . .

This should be just a *comfortable* pause. Don't do it until you are blue in the face.

3. Exhale. Exhale—but don't blow. Just let the air out through your mouth unhurriedly, saying to yourself, *Easy . . . easy . . . easy . . . easy.*

Let out as much air as you can, down to the lower part of the lungs. Feel yourself relaxing as you do: feel your shoulders, chest, and diaphragm letting go.

As you exhale, think of the tension flowing out of you.

Don't worry if the sequence isn't exact or the cadence perfect. It may seem a bit difficult to stay with at first, but just keep going. The important thing is to establish the slow, relaxed breathing rate. After the ten cycles, your breathing rate will be automatically slower and you can dispense with the "one and two and three and four" cadence.

Now do as follows:

4. Inhale. Breathe in fully.

5. Hold breath. Hold it very briefly.

6. Exhale. Let the air out slowly (don't blow), saying mentally, *Easy . . . easy . . . easy . . . easy* with each exhalation.
Repeat this cycle ten more times.

You will soon begin to feel a calm, thoroughly pleasurable feeling—some say a warmth—radiating from your chest throughout your body.

Now do as follows:

7. Tell yourself relaxing phrases. Following the second ten cycles, let yourself breathe normally and tell yourself relaxing phrases: *I feel very relaxed. . . . All the tension is going out of me as I exhale and good feelings are coming into me as I inhale. . . . When I am playing my sport, I will be able to take a few deep breaths and by saying, "Easy", will be able to tell myself to relax whenever I feel overly tense. . . . When I'm playing, I will recall the good feelings I am experiencing now and they will automatically return to me.* Imagine all this happening as you say it to yourself.

Now do as follows:

8. Inhale. Breathe in slowly.

9. Hold breath. Hold it very briefly.

10. Exhale. Let the air out slowly while mentally saying to yourself, *Easy . . . easy . . . easy . . . easy.*
Repeat this cycle ten times.

Following the third ten cycles again let your breathing go naturally, and pay attention to the pleasant feelings in your body. Repeat the same encouraging phrases to yourself that you did earlier. Listen to the sound of your own breath coming in and out. You will notice that the breathing is slow and deep without your having to make it that way. The exhaling will last longer—as long as an eight-count, perhaps.

Continue to do the breathing exercises for the rest of the session, each time alternating the ten cycles of inhale-hold-exhale with the mental encouragement.

After the last cycle of ten, just let yourself enjoy the relaxed feeling for a minute. Tell yourself, *For the rest of the day I will recall these sensations every time I tell myself, "Easy."*

It is most important that you not try to force yourself to huff and puff or to take huge gulps of air. You'll be defeating the relaxation effect if you do. Your aim should be to have the breathing feel natural. As you become more and more relaxed, such breathing will be virtually effortless and you'll feel as if the air were coming in and out of its own accord. This effect will start to become more pronounced after the third or fourth day of the exercise.

The "Breathing Easy" approach won't work if you try to rush it. As you learn and practice it, stay with what you are doing in the here and now. Pay close attention to the air coming in when you inhale, to the feelings of fullness when you hold it, and to the feelings of release when you exhale. Don't be trying to catch up with what you will be doing next. The whole effect embodied in this technique is one of slowing yourself down.

Practice the "Getting Loose" and "Breathing Easy" exercises for a total of 20 minutes each day. By the end of the second week, you will experience greater relaxation than when you first started.

Now let us go on to the third week of preparation.

THE THIRD WEEK: SPORTS PSYCHING TECHNIQUE NO. 3— "STAYING ON THE BALL"

Concentration is when you are "on" your best game.

When Jim Brown was at Syracuse University, a reporter once spotted him sitting alone in the stadium before the start of a game. Brown was staring off into space. "What are you doing?" the reporter asked.

"Thinking about football," Brown answered.

What was he, specifically, thinking about football? Running, blocking, pass patterns?

"No," said Brown. "Just about the word: 'football.' "

Brown was practicing the art of *concentration*. He was focusing attention on a single thing for a given time and preparing himself to apply that focus during the game.

The anecdotes about concentration in sport are endless. Ilie Nastase is one of the most emotionally uncontrolled players in all of professional sports, but after winning a recent Masters tennis tournament with a display of coolness and precision that he had never shown on the courts before, he said, "I am 29 and I only concentrated twice in my life: once was yesterday against Guillermo Villas and the other time was today, against Borg. I think I'll try to keep like this. I realize now that it's good for my game." And Julius Irving has said, "You know, the perfect player—and there aren't any—is the guy who can maintain his concentration 100 percent of the time he is playing. The longer you play and the more experience you have, the closer you can come to that 100 percent."

Sportscasters often tell us that great athletes going into action are the "picture of perfect concentration." Without concentration, coaches say, no athlete can be successful. No one now needs to be convinced of its importance. Players, coaches, and commentators are unanimous. Concentration is the key to the kingdom of athletic excellence. It is a key that each of us only rarely uses in a systematic way. But we can.

There has been a great deal of publicity recently about individual athletes (Joe Namath, for example) who use Transcendental Meditation for relaxation and concentration, as well as for some other goals. Four major league baseball teams—Chicago, Pittsburgh, Detroit, and Philadelphia—are reported to have officially sponsored programs. The physiological goals of TM, the lessening of stress and the calming of the inner spirit, are obviously of value to an athlete who plays a highly competitive game. Other disciplines, such as Zen and yoga, also have relaxation, concentration, and meditation techniques that could be of value in sports. The TM proponents, however, are critical of Zen and yoga, claiming their way is "natural" and easily accessible whereas the benefits of the other techniques "show up clearly only after fifteen or twenty-five years of practice." The pros and cons of these various schools are outside our range of discussion here, and in any case it is my feeling that most of the measurable physiological benefits that an athlete can gain from these disciplines can be derived from our Sports Psyching exercises. The TM, Zen, and yoga techniques of concentration are aimed at a different level of "cosmic consciousness" than is needed by most athletes. We are mainly interested in developing your ability to eliminate extraneous thoughts that distract you when you play.

What "Staying on the Ball" Is

It might be wise to start by saying what concentration is not. Concentration is not contemplating. Contemplation is a thinking process, an analytical process in which one considers not only what is, but what has been, and what may be. The aim of contemplating is primarily intellectual enrichment of one's understanding of the contemplated object. In concentration, however, the past and the future fall away as one comes in contact with the object and experiences the object, and *only* the object, of concentration in the Now.

None of this is as mysterious as it may sound. We all know the experience of being fascinated by something, of being held spellbound, just as we also know that the mind is often a gypsy, constantly moving, shifting from one stimulus to another, keeping us from fully committing our energies to one act. What the exercises will do is help you avoid being distracted by inside and outside elements during competition and expand the length of time you can concentrate on a single activity.

Concentration is a natural function of the mind. It is the focusing of your attention on one image, object, experience, task, or line of thought as it is taking place. When you concentrate, you exclude anything not pertinent to the subject of your attention. For example, you may be so absorbed in doing a crossword puzzle (or, I hope, in reading this book) you won't hear someone call you from the next room. Or so absorbed in a movie you are oblivious to the person next to you getting up and leaving.

Such exclusion is a natural proclivity; it is the way we sort out the stimuli around us. We put them into patterns (called Gestalts) and pay attention to one pattern at a time. It's a lot less confusing that way—and besides we don't have much choice in the matter because that's the way our brains

work. The familiar perception trick of the silhouetted vase demonstrates this exclusion process. Most of us first see a vase, outlined in the middle. Then we see two identical human profiles face to face, as our attention switches from the center to the outside portions of the drawing. We don't see both vase and faces at once.

The main difference between concentrating and simply having your attention on something for the moment is that concentration is deliberate and controlled and does not move from one object to the next. Lack of concentration is partly why we often miss the easy shots; we have too much time to make them, and frequently two or three alternative actions occur to us and when we try to do all of them simultaneously we miss. (The distraction of having too much time is well recognized by professional athletes. For instance, calling time out just before the other team makes a field goal attempt gives the kicker an opportunity to think about the kick and to feel the pressure on him.)

In sports, concentration is more difficult than under ordinary circumstances, for it usually must be done under pressure. Pressure can cause anxiety, and anxiety is a distraction. And the higher the anxiety, the shakier the concentration. When you feel anxiety, your worries, doubts, anger, frustration, self-consciousness, and discouragement tend to crowd your attention and, because your mind pays attention to only one thing at a time, pushes out the things you were trying to concentrate on. Furthermore, the feelings of those emotions—the feedback of "fight or flight"—tend to be more compelling to your imagination than the cool, rational actions on which you had intended to focus attention.

You concentrate best, then, when you are *relaxed*. If you are reading a book for fun or enjoying a show or pursuing a hobby, you don't feel you have to prove anything. And so, without even knowing it, at those moments, your powers of concentration are very deep. And it is the same in sports. As professional bowler Ray Mitchell says, "relaxed concentration"—that state of calm, focused attention—is "most important of all to superior performance."

What "Staying on the Ball" Does

Every sport requires you to fix your concentration on something. In most sports—golf, tennis, baseball, volleyball, Ping-pong, for example—you have to keep your eye on the ball, and that is why I call this particular technique "Staying on the Ball." Rod Laver gives this advice to aspiring tennis champions: "In concentrating you have to wipe everything out of your mind but . . . the ball. Nothing but the ball. Glue your eyes on it. Marry it. Don't let it get out of your sight. Never mind your opponent, the weather, or anything. Nothing but the ball. Make that ball an obsession. If you can get yourself into that trance, pressure won't intrude. It's just you and the ball."

What our concentration technique does is make it easier for you to get yourself into "that trance." You focus your attention on something long enough to become more aware of how total concentration feels. At the same time you increase your ability to do this in a more controlled and deliberate way. In other words you'll be better able to control your powers of concentration during a game by being better able to recognize swiftly when your concentration is off and being able to get yourself back into that state quickly.

I once knew an excellent college basketball center whose game was superior in every way except at the free-throw line. During play he couldn't sink a shot from the line, although he would always do well during practice. His trouble was self-consciousness, something he developed as a youth because of his extraordinary height and which unconsciously returned whenever he stood alone at the free-throw line with everyone watching him. He was able to overcome much of this by mentally practicing, keeping his eyes glued to the basketball rim. He would sit by himself before every game and imagine the rim for several minutes, concentrating totally on the image of it. Then, at the free-throw line during a game, just looking at the rim would help get him immediately into total concentration on it, allowing him to forget his self-consciousness.

Concentrating on the actions you can control in the game—on meeting intrinsic challenges—prevents you from thinking about things that are beyond your control and that are going to cause distracting anxieties. When you do this, energies that could have been dissipated into distracting emotions are channeled into the task at hand. Because you can pay attention to only one thing at a time, by extension you can respond to only one thing—in this case, the play to which you can commit yourself fully.

The better you concentrate, then, the better you seem to play. You become more alert to what is happening around you, because your attention is now undivided. And because you are mentally "there" for more elapsed time than if your mind were wandering, time indeed seems to slow down. You literally feel that you have more time to perform the necessary motions because you are with the activity all *its* time. Indeed many athletes become so good at concentration that they say they can tell where the ball is going to be before it gets there with a degree of certainty that they never had before.

This expansion of time is one of the great joys of sports; it feels great to be fully concentrating on the action. These are the feelings of emotional release, euphoria, involvement, and elation that mark our high points in sports. They are what we go out there for. Those positive feelings also reinforce your concentration by captivating your attention, which in turn spurs you to commit yourself more fully to the action–to really get into the play and enjoy it–giving you that feeling of release that always comes when you are "on" your game.

Learning to "Stay on the Ball"

Concentration in sports isn't knitting your brow and straining to pay attention. It is, first of all, being in the natural, relaxed state of mind you experienced in the "Getting Loose" and "Breathing Easy" exercises–especially the latter technique, in which the cadence count helps narrow your attention to your own breathing. Indeed, the act of doing the exercises is itself an example of concentration, for you zeroed in your attention to the procedures and their pleasant sensation.

Thus, during this third week you will continue to practice the relaxation techniques, both to improve your ability to relax and as initial steps for concentration. Ultimately, you will be able to reduce the time it takes to get yourself into relaxation, so that by the end of this six-week program you can relax yourself in just a few moments by use of the cue words.

The "Staying on the Ball" technique will help you put the act of concentration on a more conscious, deliberate level and eventually help you to better control your ability to concentrate fully during those moments in your game when you need it most. There are two aspects to the technique: (1) you limit your attention in space (that is, narrow your concentration to one area or thing) and (2) you limit it in time (you are conscious only of the present), for when you are concentrating in sports you must be in the here and now.

Very simply, this exercise is comprised of concentrating on one thing for a brief period of time, learning to shut everything else out of your consciousness, just as Jim Brown was doing with the word, "football." At the beginning it is best to have a real object on which to focus your attention, such as a small glass, matchbook, or pencil. Or better still some object that is a part of your game, something on which you must concentrate during play, such as a tennis ball or golf ball.

Even a photograph of the object will do—for example, a large, clear picture of a bowling alley with pins set up or of the racing lanes in an Olympic pool—but it is best to begin with a physical object. In yoga concentration exercises, breathing or one's heartbeat is frequently the object of concentration. One can learn as well to concentrate on a sound such as the ticking of a clock. For the sake of demonstration, we will use a ball as the object of concentration as we describe the exercise.

The point of having an object is not to give you some deeper mysterious knowledge of your sport but rather to facilitate the concentration technique. A javelin thrower or a swimmer needs to develop his powers of concentration just as much as a golf or tennis player, and *it is the learning of concentration techniques and not the object* that is important here. Now, let us begin the technique.

Set aside 20 minutes a day, just as you did the previous week. However, this time, instead of lying down, sit at a desk or table. Put the ball or other object of concentration in front of you.

Do the "Getting Loose" exercise, but in the following, less elaborate way: Simply sit back as comfortably as you can and *think* your way through the sequence of muscles, without doing the tensing-relaxing part of it. Just say to the muscles in your left leg, *Let go . . . let go,* starting with the lower leg, then doing the same for the upper leg. Jiggle the leg slightly and tense the muscles just a little, and then let go.

Don't be concerned with how deeply you are relaxing the leg. You are not trying to reach the deep state of relaxation you could achieve lying down. You are only trying to rid yourself of any excess tension you might have and put yourself at ease. By now the cue phrase, *Let go*, should have the effect of automatically letting excess tension go out of you. You are gradually working up to the point where you will be able to do this just before and during breaks in a game.

Now tell your right leg, *Let go*. Repeat the procedure for buttocks and thighs, stomach, back and neck, arms and shoulders, jaw, face, and eyes.

With your eyes closed, do ten of the "Breathing Easy" exercises, just as you did the previous week. Breathe in slowly to a count of four. Hold for four and exhale slowly, saying to yourself, *Easy . . . easy . . . easy . . . easy*.

At this point you should feel thoroughly calm. If you still feel some residual tension—perhaps because it may have been a particularly trying day for you—do another ten "Breathing Easy" exercises. But don't push it beyond that. You are not in a contest to see how relaxed you can get: you simply want to be relaxed enough so that you can narrow your attention and start concentrating.

Now begin the concentration exercise, which should take 10 minutes, as follows:

1. **Say concentration word.** Open your eyes and look at the ball. Say to yourself, *Ball*. The repetition of a word helps to keep the mind from wandering. If you are not in a ball-oriented sport, as you concentrate on the chosen object or picture say a short, soft, nondistracting word—e.g., *one,*

run, goal, lane, arm—that will help you to focus on that object or picture.

2. Examine the object of concentration. Now begin to examine the ball visually in every detail. Look at its outline, at its surface. Is it rough or smooth? Does it have seams, dimples, printing on it? Are there scratches or scuff marks? Look at its colors and how the light and shadows fall on its surface. Don't try to hold your gaze unblinking. Relax.

3. Feel the object. Pick up the ball. Feel its texture. Turn it around and look at it from various angles.

4. Imagine the object. Put the ball down and focus your mind and eyes on it. See the ball as fully as you can so that its smallest detail will stand out in your mind. Know the ball. "Marry it." Don't try to overpower the object of your concentration. As you relax and simply keep your eye on it, you will find that the object will seem to "come to you." You must maintain something of a passive attitude in this process, allowing the object of your concentration to enter into your mind fully and not simply be something external that you are studying. When you concentrate, you will find that this seemingly mysterious process happens quite naturally.

5. Get the feeling. When your concentration breaks, as it will, say to yourself: *I have been concentrating on the ball. . . . This is what it feels like to be concentrating. . . . I am relaxed, I feel good, my attention is totally focused on the ball. . . . This is concentration.* Look back at the ball.

6. Again say concentration word. Now say to yourself, *Ball.* Look at the ball. Concentrate.

7. **"Breathing Easy."** Close your eyes and do ten more of the "Breathing Easy" exercises.

The first time you try this "Staying on the Ball" technique, and many times thereafter, you'll find your mind won't stay on the ball. A wide variety of unrelated outside thoughts will come to your attention, and you will become aware of body messages or noises from the street or the next room. Don't despair. Simply bring your mind back to the object of your concentration and keep repeating the word. When, as it will, your mind wanders once again, gently return it once more to the object. As you work on this, you will find that your mind stays with the object for longer and longer periods and that quite simply your powers of concentration grow as you use them with some conscious technique.

Practice the above technique every day. At the end of one week, you will be able to concentrate for a longer period than when you started—not for two minutes at a time, not even for one, unless you're very good at this, but still, it will be longer than what you used to do.

Naturally, you are not going to go through such an elaborate routine to achieve relaxed concentration once you begin to use these Sports Psyching techniques in your game itself. But this is the most effective way of building up your *experience* of the state of relaxed concentration in the beginning.

Continue these exercises for the fourth, fifth, and sixth weeks of the program. As you do them you will find relaxed concentration coming to you more easily and readily. Finally, you will be able to put yourself into a relaxed state just using a deep breath and the cue words. Saying, *Let go,* will rid yourself of tension, *Easy* will start the relaxation process, and *Ball* will focus your attention and shut out inner and outer distractions.

All that will be left for you to face, then, will be the intrinsic challenges of the game itself—which are, after all, the only ones that you can do something about.

PRACTICE: 10
Overlearning to Avoid Underplaying

Rehearsal makes Sports Psyching a habit.

To improve your game is to change. It is to replace one habit with another.

But you can't change habits while you are playing. In fact, you can't even be *thinking* about what you want to do: your full attention has to be on the here and now, on the action of the play itself. When the serve is whizzing into your court you have to react to it automatically. You can't be telling yourself, "Don't be intimidated now," or, "Watch how you move your feet." Your reaction must be automatic, the response you have learned best.

However, because most recreational athletes don't get out to practice and play as often as do career athletes, they have difficulty consistently coming up with correctly executed plays. They tend to forget details in techniques, or they get them wrong and slip easily into improper habits. The point of this chapter, then, is to help you make that automatic reaction a *desirable* reaction.

The best way to establish this desirable behavior is by overlearning it. When something has been overlearned, it is so habitual that you can do it without thinking about it—like driving a car.

THE FOURTH AND FIFTH WEEKS: SPORTS PSYCHING TECHNIQUE NO. 4— MENTAL REHEARSAL

Making the desirable patterns automatic.

Mental Rehearsal is used by many athletes. Dodger catcher Joe Ferguson and Rams lineman Charlie Cowan are two who say that before a game they methodically go over in their minds all the plays they are likely to see and then mentally rehearse their responses to them. Jack Nicklaus does it, too. He calls it "going to the movies." He says that he imagines each shot from start to finish before he actually makes it—mentally setting up, swinging, hitting the ball, seeing it take off, land, and roll to a stop. Dr. Richard Suinn, a psychologist with the American ski team for the 1976 Winter Olympics, has taught mental rehearsal to several skiers, with great success.

What Mental Rehearsal Is

Mental Rehearsal is not Walter Mitty daydreaming. It is a drill that calls for precision and puts you to work on setting correct moves and strategies firmly into your athletic repertoire. It is the technique you will learn in the next two weeks to make sure the habits you want are the strongest ones. It is a powerful psychological tool that allows you to take what you would most *like* to do and turn it into what you will most *likely* do.

The technique should not be confused with wishful thinking or even positive thinking. Wishful thinking is fantasizing about something you hope is coming true but over which you have little control. Positive thinking is telling yourself you can do it. Both are concerned with ends rather than with means: you're either hoping for the best or you're attempting to build enough self-confidence to do your best. With Mental Rehearsal, on the other hand, you are thinking and practicing the doing, the means by which you can give your best possible performance.

Mental Rehearsal is an extension of the natural way we plan our actions in everyday life. Say you want to get your tennis racquet or bowling ball out of the closet. Ordinarily you wouldn't tell yourself verbally, "Go to the closet, open the door, locate it, grasp it, pull it out, close the door," and so on. Instead, you simply decide to do it, your body gets the message and then goes and does it. The computer that is your nervous system has already been programmed and it automatically throws the right switches to take appropriate action. But with Mental Rehearsal you are doing this "programming" in a more deliberate way. You are saying to your nervous system, "Here's what I'll be wanting you to do."

The instructions you give yourself are presented in images, for whenever you learn a sports skill in words (from a book or someone's explanations) you have to translate it into images for your body to carry it out. The more vivid and detailed the image, the better your body can understand what it has to do. This is one of the reasons why just watching someone playing well can improve the quality of your own performance. Because Mental Rehearsal gives you sufficient practice imagining yourself making a play, your muscles will subtly respond to your thoughts during a game and simulate the motions just below their threshold of action without your being aware of it.

What Mental Rehearsal Does

Mental Rehearsal is an extension of the relaxation-concentration process. It extends concentration in that it carries your focused attention right into the upcoming action and keeps it there. It is a way of getting used to keeping your mind in the here and now as you go through the sports action.

This helps reduce generalized anxieties, shutting them out of your consciousness. You replace thoughts both positive and negative about the result of the previous play or nervousness about the outcome of the next with the mental rehearsal of the successful play. You replace something out of your control—hoping that all will go well somehow—with positive action to control the situation by practicing the moves you want to make and giving yourself the best possible chance of doing them the right way.

It is most important, therefore, that you always mentally rehearse the *correct* action, imagine the *successful* play, no matter how much uncertainty, trepidation, or false modesty tempt you. For if you mentally rehearse a failed play, you will be reinforcing the *wrong* actions, with all the negative emotions that go along with them. Concentrating on what you must not do—hit the ball into the trap, give the net man an easy shot, whatever—as often as not prepares the body for just those actions you want to avoid. Thus, you must always think about what you want to do and mentally rehearse only the desired action.

The imagined result of mentally rehearsing a play as coming off favorably may give you the positive thinking bonus of bolstering confidence, but this is not the important part. The important thing is for you to rehearse *how* you make the successful play—the correct motions and strategies. You are using it to overlearn the action and make it so familiar that under pressure you are most likely to do it automatically because it has become the most familiar and compelling of your responses.

Mental Rehearsal will help you cope with emotional stress as well as improve physical proficiency. Because the key to dealing with emotional stress is to divert your attention and energies into your best efforts to make the play, you can mentally rehearse accomplishing this under pressure, especially under those pressures that affect you most. This is where what you have learned about your responses in the SERP will help. Using your self-scouting information, you can pinpoint those situations that cause you the most anxiety in athletics. Now you will mentally rehearse being able to fully concentrate on making the play and shutting out the anxieties you find most distracting.

The fourth week of the Sports Psyching program will be devoted to rehearsing mentally the basic physical skill moves of your game. In the fifth week, you will mentally rehearse the same plays, but this time imagining yourself gradually under increasing pressure in the situations that tend to rattle you the most. By the end of these two weeks you will be able to go through these plays in your imagination and greatly reduce the pressure you feel. You will be well on the way toward being able to do this in actual play.

**Learning Mental Rehearsal—
The Fourth Week**

Set aside your 20 minutes per day in private. Seat yourself at a desk or table. Put the ball or equipment in front of you. Now choose some basic part of your game you wish to rehearse, based on the results of the Physical Self-Scouting Survey, which have shown you the particular parts of your game you feel need most improvement. As you did in that survey, break the parts of your move or play down into details. This is important now, because when you mentally rehearse it you want to be sure you are including all the components of the movement.

Get a set of photos or drawings of the particular play in front of you; these pictures can be found in most instruction books. Or, if you don't have pictures immediately available, write down the parts of the play in as much detail as you can. The box shows a very detailed description—far more than I would expect any recreational athlete to accomplish—of how this could be done for a 5-iron swing.

EXAMPLE OF HOW TO BREAK DOWN THE PARTS OF PLAY OF A 5-IRON SWING

Grip. Hands properly aligned so that back of left hand and front of right face desired direction of ball. "Vees" formed at thumbs point over shoulders; grasp is strongest between thumb and first two fingers of each hand, but not too tight. Stick is held so that club face is at right angle to intended shot direction and so that it meets the ball dead center.

Stance. Feet are proper distance apart, knees slightly bent, weight slightly to the inside of each foot. Ball is proper distance away and aligned a few inches back from the inside of front foot. A line drawn from toe to toe should point in the direction you wish to hit ball. Arms straight. Head down; eyes on the ball, looking to the rear half of it.

Backswing. Legs and hips begin to rotate: shoulders turn until hips approach a forty-five-degree angle (or as close as possible to it). Weight shifts mainly to inside of rear foot, as front knee flexes and turns inward; left foot is raised slightly with weight on toes. Shoulders approach a ninety-degree angle to what they were at address. Meanwhile, arms and hands pull club back so club head describes a low arc away from ball gradually coming up. Left arm stays straight and right elbow bends, taking care to keep it tucked close to your side. Wrists

---

Before you start the Mental Rehearsal, go over your materials a few times to review the sequence of action briefly in your mind. Do this even if the play is thoroughly familiar. Refresh your memory on the fundamentals; even pros allow mistakes to creep into their games, and review them often to weed out errors. Golf instructor Irv Schloss, winner of the United States Golf Association's Horton Smith Award, urges this method of mental rehearsal for his students. "There is a high rate of forgetting in the learning

---

are cocked after taking the club upwards, but not back behind you. Head stays immobile as possible, eyes on the ball and neck serving as axis of swing.

Downswing. Legs and hips start rotation back the other way. Simultaneously, body comes around and arms start downswing, with wrists starting to uncock about halfway down. It is important to rotate hips rather than let them sway laterally. Weight moves from inside of back foot to the squared stance you had at address, the weight roughly equal on each foot. As club head comes through the ball, you are almost exactly at the middle position you were at address. Both arms are straight, the head is down, eyes on the ball.

Follow-through. The club head's momentum carries it through the ball. Weight shifts to the inside of front (left) foot, with that leg remaining locked while the back (right) knee flexes forward and inward. Arms and hands remain straight as they follow the arc upward. Hips and shoulders turn toward direction of the ball, and only then does head begin to turn forward. Follow-through should be full, with club head describing as much of a vertical arc as possible from backswing through impact and follow-through. It is as if you swing a weight hooked to a wire, building up centrifugal force. Club ends up cocked loosely over left shoulder.

---

of any motor skill," he says, "and for this reason, if the golfer has a set of reminders in front of him showing him the sequence in which he should be thinking of things, it will be very valuable."

Begin the first half of the 20-minute exercise, as follows:

First do the "Getting Loose" and "Breathing Easy" exercises, as before, only do them for five minutes. Then do the "Staying on the Ball" routine for another five minutes. Look at the ball (or whatever) and concentrate until your mind is staying with the object. Set the ball aside.

Now begin the Mental Rehearsal exercise, which will take 10 minutes:

1. **Study the pictures**. Study the pictures or your list for a few moments, going through the entire sequence a couple of times.

2. **Imagine the sequence in slow motion**. Close your eyes and imagine yourself going through the same sequence. Imagine this in slow motion. Note the crucial components of each stage of the actions—where your feet are; what your legs are doing; what your hips, back, arms, are doing; where your head is; what your grip or hand motions are. Imagine the sensations; check how each part of your body feels— where your balance is, how, when, and where strength is applied. Imagine what you see when you make the play. If you are supposed to be looking at a ball, then see where it goes from start of play to end of play—a racquet making contact, a ball bouncing, and so on.

3. **Study and imagine the sequence again**. Now look at the pictures or list again. See if you missed anything or got

anything wrong. If so, correct it. Now imagine the action with your eyes closed again, in slow motion.

4. **Repeat sequence five times in more detail.** Repeat this procedure five times, each time in more detail, looking at your reminders, and then closing your eyes and imagining yourself doing this. Always imagine the play from start to successful conclusion. Bring out the feeling, sharpen up the image. Keep checking your reminders to keep motions correct. When you can go slowly through the action, start to finish, smoothly in detail, without error, then you've "got the picture." You may not be able to reach this point the first time you try it. If so, don't pressure yourself about it. It won't be long before you have it.

5. **Imagine the sequence at normal speed ten times.** Close your eyes and this time imagine yourself going through the play at normal speed. Imagine the play is the best you have performed. Imagine it through from start to finish, and say to yourself, *That was a terrific play.* Check over your reminders—the pictures or list—close your eyes and repeat your "best play" again. Do this ten times.

Repeat this Mental Rehearsal routine each day during the fourth week. The relaxation and concentration exercises should take about 10 minutes and the Mental Rehearsal about 10 minutes.

Learning Mental Rehearsal— The Fifth Week

During this week, the purpose of the exercise is to rehearse overcoming pressure while continuing to go through the action properly.

Begin the first half of the 20-minute exercise, as follows:

Start with two minutes of "Getting Loose" and "Breathing Easy" and do three minutes of "Staying on the Ball." Then mentally rehearse the play you practiced the fourth week—five times in slow motion, then five (not ten) times at normal speed. This should take about another five minutes.

Check back over your SERP results, then think of a situation in sports that generally is a problem. If you scored too high on Desire, then think of a sports situation in which you generally become anxious because you are expecting too much of yourself. If you scored low on Assertiveness, think of a situation in which you are letting yourself become intimidated by a showy opponent. If your problem area is Sensitivity, think of a situation where you have fallen behind and your opponent is making sure to point it out. If it's low on Tension Control, imagine a situation in which your anxiety is starting to get out of hand, say after you have had a couple of plays go wrong because of bad luck. If it's low on Confidence, think of yourself in a tough situation where you will have to play your best to get out, or of getting cold feet at the start of a game because you don't feel good enough. If it's high on Personal Accountability, think of a situation where you may have just made an error and would ordinarily feel terrible about it. If you had a problem score in Self-Discipline, think of a situation in which you might tend to be too easily discouraged and rationalize that it's no use taking care with your shot, because you aren't organized enough.

Now begin the 10-minute Mental Rehearsal, as follows:

1. **Imagine the problem area clearly.** Get the surroundings and other players in mind; think of what comments

they might make and what would be your usual reactions. Do this until you can actually feel that disruptive emotion beginning to arise.

2. Do three minutes of relaxation and concentration exercises. Do the "Getting Loose" exercise—in very abbreviated form, about one minute. Then do about one minute of "Breathing Easy." Now do "Staying on the Ball"; this should take another minute.

3. Do two minutes of Mental Rehearsal, first phase. Now mentally rehearse the play you practiced the fourth week, making it correct in all details and a successful execution of your best effort. Do it five times, in slow motion and five times at normal speed. This should take about two minutes.

4. Do five minutes of Mental Rehearsal, second phase. Imagine yourself approaching the same play again, in the emotional situation. It is vital that you imagine the emotion exactly as it occurs. As soon as you start to feel the emotion, do the relaxation exercises, the concentration exercise, and mentally rehearse the successful play again. Repeat this process ten times. This should take five minutes. Always end rehearsal of this situation doing it successfully.

Follow this routine for the rest of the week.

The point of recreating the emotion-producing situations is simple. Psychologists have found that a good way to desensitize ourselves to an emotional situation is to create it in our minds over and over again in detail until we are able to imagine it without the emotion. If you can live through the emotion-provoking situation time after time in your imagination, when you come to the situation in real life, your ability to handle it will be vastly improved. Your

SERP is therefore of particular value at this point because it will help you to identify the specific psychological areas in sports which you can now handle with Sports Psyching.

THE SIXTH WEEK: SPORTS PSYCHING TECHNIQUE NO. 5– BODY REHEARSAL

Getting so you can do it with your eyes closed.

What Body Rehearsal Is

"Shadow boxing" is a common activity among athletes— that is, "grooving" or going through the physical motions of plays to get the feeling of them. Batters fan the air before the pitch, tennis players take swipes with their racquets, golfers take practice swings. Most players may not be aware of it, but there is a sound reason for doing this, for motor skills involve learning and remembering on the part of the *body* as well as the mind. Shadow boxing reinforces the correct skill motions; it upgrades what is sometimes called the "muscle sense" of a play.

Most players, however, don't do this in a way in which they could gain best advantage from it. Their practice cuts are not tied into a broader practice routine encompassing both mental and physical factors which can be used both on and off the field. Conventional practice rituals also tend to overemphasize the visual aspects; we pay more attention to whether we showed the correct form, direction, and moves rather than how the play felt. We therefore neglect that muscle sense development that is inherent in shadow-boxing routines.

Body Rehearsal, the last Sports Psyching technique, is the final step in getting you away from the distracting cultural and personal pressures that cause emotional problems in sports. It gets you fully into meeting the intrinsic challenges with your best effort.

What Body Rehearsal Does

The importance of developing muscle sense has been known among psychologists for some time. One experiment was conducted in 1952 by the late Lloyd Percival, director of Toronto's Sports College and president of the Fitness Institute there. Percival based his study on the observations of Coleman R. Griffith, a psychologist who said that most basketball players depended too much on sight when shooting and not enough on sensory feedback from their muscles. To check this hypothesis, Percival picked two groups of college basketball players, all with equal shooting ability (they averaged 20 to 21 baskets in 50 attempts). During a four-week program, the first group of players practiced predetermined shots in the conventional way, for 20 minutes each session. The second group of players practiced the same shots for the same amount of time as follows: first they shot for five minutes with eyes open; then they shot for 10 minutes blindfolded from the same spot, guided by an observer who told them where each shot went and who urged them to pay attention to their muscle sensations; and finally they shot for five minutes without blindfolds. At the end of four weeks, the first group was able to sink an average of 23 out of 50 attempts. But the second group of players, with their muscle-sense experience, had raised its average to 39 out of 50—significantly higher, in fact, than averages of most college basketball teams.

Obviously, the expression, "I can do it with my eyes closed," has a basis in reality. When you block out vision, you isolate the inner physical sensations of a play; you learn how a successful play feels as well as looks. This also reinforces your memory of it and enables you to duplicate it more easily under pressure. Moreover, it builds your confidence in making the correct plays because of your increased familiarity of them. It is an important step toward overlearning.

Learning Body Rehearsal

Continue to set aside your 20 minutes per day, only for this week, find a spot where you can go through some practice motions—your backyard or garage or a large play room will do, or perhaps a quiet spot in a park. Make sure you are in a private, nonthreatening environment, since it's important to learn this technique, like the others, free from outside distractions.

If your sport involves equipment—clubs, racquet, bat, ball, or whatever—have it with you. Obviously, certain sports won't allow this: for example, you probably won't want to roll your bowling ball in your garage. But you can go through the motions of bowling without the ball during this week and still achieve good results. And the moves of certain team sports can be practiced alone or on a field or court that's not crowded, with the same benefits.

Begin the first half of the 20-minute session:

First do a few "Getting Loose" exercises for a minute, then a few "Breathing Easy" exercises. You need only do two or three of them, but if you still feel a bit tense after that, do several more, until you feel the relaxation effect. This need take only about two minutes in all.

Then do the "Staying on the Ball" exercise—only this time just close your eyes for a few seconds, visualize the ball, and say the word to yourself—*Ball.* Then go right into the Mental Rehearsal—both slow motion and normal speed—

of the successful play you practiced during the fourth week. This should take about three minutes.

Now recreate your emotional situation, as you did in the fifth week, in your imagination and then do the relaxation techniques again as soon as the tension starts to be felt. This takes about two minutes.

Now tell yourself to concentrate and mentally rehearse the play, again in slow motion. This takes about three minutes.

Now begin the Body Rehearsal, which should take 10 minutes, as follows:

1. **Make play in slow motion, eyes open.** If you're using equipment, now is the time to pick it up. Physically go through the play—but slowly, at about half the normal speed. As you do so, check your body positions. See that your feet, legs, hips, back, shoulders, arms, hands, head move correctly. Go through the play a couple of times until you can complete it smoothly, with all details correct.

2. **Make play in slow motion, eyes closed.** Now go through the play again in slow motion, this time with your eyes closed. As you do so, pay close attention to how part of your body feels, to how the motion goes, where your balance is, when and where muscle power is applied.

3. **Correct play in slow motion, eyes open, then eyes closed, ten times.** Go through the slow-motion play again, this time with eyes open. Chances are the first time you did it with your eyes closed it felt a bit strange and you may have had trouble keeping balance or accomplishing it in a comprehensive, smooth manner. Now is the time to correct, doing it with eyes open. Now repeat it with eyes closed, then again with eyes open, each time following the same

procedure as above. Do this a total of ten times with eyes closed and ten times with eyes open. Pause briefly each time you go through the slow-motion play, and think on how you moved and how it felt.

4. Make play at normal speed, eyes open, then closed, ten times. Do ten sets eyes open and ten sets eyes closed at normal speed. Freeze during the third or fourth set and check yourself to see that all details of your body position are correct. If you are practicing throwing a shot put, for example, stop just before push-off and check the positions of your shoulders, arms, hips, and so on. If they are not in the correct position, think over how you got out of position and do another *slow motion* set to get it right before you recommence the regular speed sets.

Practice this routine each day for this final week.

This completes the six-week Sports Psyching program. You now have five techniques for coping with the pressures of any game and the emotions you may feel and for redirecting your energies into the game itself.

As we will show in the next chapter, each Sports Psyching technique can be used in both elaborate and simplified form. You can get into deep relaxation and concentration, and mental and body rehearsals, as you did during these six weeks, or you can cue yourself into them briefly. You are now able to get a lot more mileage out of your pre-game moves, for instead of simply going through the normal shadow boxing, practice swings, or whatever, you can go through a complete routine that takes into account all the emotional, mental, and physical challenges of your game.

11

PLAY:
Sports Psyching All of the Time

Letting Sports Psyching do its work.

At this point the overlearning you have achieved takes over. When you know fully what to do, you don't have to think about doing it. It almost does itself; it takes place without conscious effort on your part. So, just as you drive a car without having to think about steering, braking, and changing gears, you should be able to execute the moves of your game without consciously directing them. As Yogi Berra once said, "Ya can't t'ink 'n' hit at da same time." You've done your thinking; now hit. It is time to place your trust in the techniques. You can't be wondering, "Am I relaxed enough?" or "Did I do it right?" It's too late for that. Let Sports Psyching do its work. If you've prepared and practiced, you won't have to think about anything else.

The Sports Psyching techniques are like any other skills: the more you use them, the more effective they will become. It is not always easy to take techniques one has learned at home and apply them directly on the athletic field. Thus, when you incorporate these techniques into the actual pressure circumstances, you can expect that they will not "work" as well as they did the last time you practiced them at home. And no matter how practiced you become with these techniques, sometimes you will get better results than at other times. Don't worry about it. Sports Psyching doesn't have to work perfectly to work at all. After all, even partial relaxation and concentration is better than none.

The main thing is for you to decide to make Sports Psyching part of your game. Set yourself two goals. First, decide that for the next four weeks you will practice the techniques every day, to reach a total of ten weeks' experience in Sports Psyching—the amount of time it takes most persons to make a daily habit of any activity, whether calisthenics, jogging, swimming, or meditation. Second, continue to apply the techniques over the following six months. You will notice a gradual, substantial improvement in both the ease with which you employ them and in their effectiveness. As with all new types of behavior, first you learn them, then you become accustomed to employing them, then they become habitual.

Now let me show you five specific ways to use Sports Psyching.

1. THE PRE-GAME
WARM-UP ROUTINE

Getting yourself completely into the action.

The pre-game warm-up routine can take anywhere from three minutes to 20 minutes, depending on how much time you have to devote to it. It can be done while you're sitting on the bench, waiting to get on the court, before you take your practice shots or do your rallying or whatever your usual warm-up is. Here's how it works:

1. "Getting Loose." Briefly tense your legs, buttocks and thighs, stomach, back and neck, arms and shoulders, jaw, face, and eye muscles, holding each muscle briefly and telling it, *Let go.*

2. "Breathing Easy." Do two or three "Breathing Easy" exercises—inhaling, holding your breath while counting to four, then slowly exhaling while saying to yourself, *Easy . . . easy . . . easy . . . easy.*

3. "Staying on the Ball." Look at the ball, basketball rim, bowling pins, or whatever you've made your object of concentration, and say to yourself, *Ball . . . ball,* or whatever word you've been using. Do this for about a minute.

4. Mental Rehearsal. Close your eyes and in your mind picture the upcoming plays you will have to make, visualizing their successful accomplishment in slow motion. Obviously, you can't anticipate every play, but you can mentally rehearse the fundamental moves. For example, in tennis you can mentally rehearse the serve, then the several kinds of strokes you have to employ in rallying the possible return. In baseball you can rehearse the act of hitting, of how you will handle the various kinds of pitches likely to come at you.

5. Body Rehearsal. This can be done when you take the field or court and do your usual physical warm-ups. Shadow-box the moves, first with eyes closed, then with eyes open, one set in slow motion, one at normal speed.

You are now ready to commence play.

2. THE PRE-PLAY
SPORTS PSYCHING ROUTINE

Taking advantage of breaks in the action.

The pre-play or between-plays routine takes only half a minute to a minute. It should be adapted to the circumstances of your particular game. In certain sports there is time before each shot to go through this routine. With other sports, you will have to take advantage of breaks in the action—brief time-outs or while waiting for someone to retrieve a ball. The best time to do the routine is just before you are going to rejoin play, which is the time most players go through some kind of warm-up ritual anyway. Here's how it works:

1. **"Getting Loose."** Tense all your muscles briefly, then say to yourself, *Let go . . . let go,* and feel your muscles go loose.

2. **"Breathing Easy."** Take a deep breath, hold it for a four count, and let it out, saying to yourself, *Easy . . . easy . . . easy . . . easy.*

3. **"Staying on the Ball."** Look at the ball (or whatever) and say to yourself, *Ball . . . ball* (or whatever your word is).

4. **Mental Rehearsal.** Close your eyes and in your mind picture the successful play you're about to make with that ball, visualizing every move from start to finish, seeing the ball (or whatever) hit its target.

5. **Body Rehearsal.** Still keeping your eyes closed, make your practice move—swing the club, racquet, or whatever. Now make your practice move with your eyes open.

You are now ready to make the play.

3. USING SPORTS PSYCHING TO IMPROVE PHYSICAL SKILLS

Raising your percentage of "best day" plays.

Make use of the Physical Self-Scouting Survey described in Chapter 7 to find the area of your sport which you think needs work and precisely what it is you want to correct or improve about that area.

As you did in the sixth week of the program, set aside 20 minutes a day for a week in your backyard, garage, basement, or wherever you have privacy and room to move, and practice all of the Sports Psyching techniques: relax yourself, concentrate, mentally and physically rehearse the move you wish to correct or improve.

Some time the following week go to a practice area and devote an hour to practice by yourself or with someone. Go through your preparation and rehearsal techniques first, then run through the play ten times. Repeat the preparation and practice routine, then again make the play another ten times. Schedule three sessions like this first one.

Check your percentages after the last session. If there has been little or no improvement, schedule another practice session. It is most likely there will be some improvement, certainly much more than there would be with conventional practice techniques. After this, if possible, play in a low-pressure practice game. If you now feel more secure with your improved skill, you are ready to use it at your regular level of competition.

A minor correction, of course, won't take as long to accomplish as a major change. If there are stubborn problems, it is best to consult an instructor (see Chapter 13).

Remember that it is difficult to replace long-standing bad habits. Often, you'll find yourself slipping back into the old habit, especially when under pressure. If this is happening often, keep practicing the new habit privately for another week, follow it with three practice sessions, then employ it in your game. If there is only occasional backsliding, don't worry about it. Keep trying to use the new, corrected skill. The key is raising your percentage of "best day" plays. Remember, your aim is greater consistency, not perfection.

4. USING SPORTS PSYCHING TO COPE WITH PRESSURE SITUATIONS

Psyching yourself into your best.

By now you know from your SERP what kinds of situations rattle you. Think of the ways you wish to respond in those situations. Set aside 20 minutes of privacy a day for a week and imagine yourself in each situation. As soon as you begin to feel the anxiety of the situation, do the relaxation and concentration exercises, then 'the Mental Rehearsal of carrying out the play successfully. The next week, set aside 20 minutes of privacy a day for Body Rehearsal. After imagining each pressure situation, then doing the relaxation, concentration, and Mental Rehearsal exercises, do twenty sets of the Body Rehearsal—ten with eyes closed at slow motion, ten at normal speed, eyes open.

The third week perform the Sports Psyching techniques at the practice field, then put in an hour's conventional practice. Later that week arrange to play a game at a low level of competition; arrive early and do the exercises beforehand. Then the next time you are to play in a regular game, arrive early and go through the same routine before the game.

What effect will all this have on your game? Will it guarantee there won't be any pressure on you? No. You haven't been practicing to make the pressure disappear, but to learn to respond to pressure situations more constructively. As you recognize any pressure situation, you automatically will respond to it in a way that takes you away from emotion and into relaxation, concentration, rehearsing, and getting into the action.

There will be variations among individuals, of course, but most people who follow this procedure will see pressure problems significantly alleviated after two to three weeks. After this, whenever there are lapses, take advantage of breaks in the action to go through your Sports Psyching routine and do the same thing before each game. If you keep at this faithfully during the next six months, you will find that it comes automatically.

5. USING SPORTS PSYCHING FOR SPECIFIC PURPOSES

Using the techniques tactically as well as strategically.

Sports Psyching is not just a general approach to your game. It is a specific tool to apply in specific circumstances. Here are a few of them.

Preparing for the big game. Use the relaxation, concentration, and Mental Rehearsal techniques the week before that big event in order to psych yourself up for the game.

Reviewing your game. If you have laid off a sport for a while, take a week of 20-minute sessions to review the basic moves.

Rehearsing strategy. Before a game you can think out what you feel will be the most effective game plan—playing the net, pressing in the backcourt—and mentally rehearse the plays that will be required, first in slow motion, then at normal speed.

Getting used to new equipment. If you have recently purchased new equipment, it's a good idea to do a few sets of Body Rehearsal with it—first in slow motion and then at normal speed—for a few minutes each day for three or four days before using it in a game. This will help you get used to the feel of it and build your confidence in it.

Being prepared for the unfamiliar. Sports Psyching can be helpful whenever you're encountering something new to you—taking up a new sport, playing in a new area or unfamiliar territory, playing a different set of opponents than ones you're used to, or applying a new technique or strategy.

REPLAYING THE GAME IN YOUR HEAD

Getting ready for tomorrow by reviewing today

If you are developing your game, either as a beginner or as a more experienced player wishing to improve skills, you should have a constructive way of evaluating and learning from each play experience. The time to do this is after the play or after the game is over. Replay the action in your head, the same way as you mentally rehearsed, imagining yourself as you performed it.

Pick the plays you performed poorly and break them down to find the cause of the problem. If the cause was something you couldn't control, such as luck, field conditions, or the action of another player, concentrate on your emotional reaction to the situation. If it was in your control, pinpoint the reason or reasons for the faulty performance. Was the problem psychological? Were you nervous or distracted during the play? In that case, think about whether it would have helped to prepare more effectively by relaxing and concentrating. Was there an error in physical skill or strategy, a wrong move or bad positioning? If so, you might want to do some extra practice on that play, going over it the correct way with Mental Rehearsal and Body Rehearsal techniques.

You should also replay the plays in which you felt you did your best, paying special attention to recalling how they felt. This will help make those superior plays more vividly set in your imagination so you can make them more consistently part of your play repertoire. You can use the recollection of those superior plays and shots as the "script" for subsequent mental rehearsal and muscle sense rehearsal. Build up a varied collection of these positive experiences to use as models in practicing other plays of your game.

That's the works on Sports Psyching. As we've seen, it is mainly concerned with getting control of your own mind and body. But what about the effects of *others*—competitors, teammates, and coaches—on your game?

PLAYING THE ULTIMATE GAME

The emphasis of the Sports Psyching techniques has been on the practical application of psychological and physiological techniques to improving your game. I have deliberately not dealt with the much heralded spiritual attributes that many athletes derive from sports. A good deal has been written about this experience, and three books describe it with particular clarity and excitement: *Zen in the Art of Archery*, by Eugen Herrigel, *The Inner Game of Tennis*, by W. Timothy Gallwey, and *The Ultimate Athlete* by George Leonard. If you are able to accomplish the fully relaxed concentration I describe above, you, too, may find that you will be able to enjoy that meaningful inner experience.

12

YOUR GAME AND THEIR GAMES:
Psych-outs and How to Avoid Them

Behind most games there is the psychological contest in which no one wins.

You are always playing two games at once. The first game is objective. It presents a physical challenge—achieving a goal by overcoming obstacles within the rules or framework of the sport—e.g., trying to move the ball from tee to hole in so many strokes. The second game is psychological—the ego game. In it, symbolic, personal value is attributed to the accomplishment of physical tasks in the sport. It is exemplified by the expression, "May the better man win," which inflates the meaning of victory from the simple decision of who played more effectively in the game to a verdict on which person is superior.

The ego game can include worrying about how you look, wanting to put down another player, feeling guilty about succeeding, being afraid of hurting someone else's feelings, striving for recognition or social acceptance, making sports a yardstick for self-esteem, and so on. Much casual betting by weekend athletes also is a psychological game. The money isn't important except as a symbol of reward and punishment, a tangible homage loser pays to winner in the postgame ceremony at the clubhouse bar.

COMPETITION AND
THE EGO GAME

Becoming too involved in ego games can make a shambles of your physical game.

There are players who enjoy ego games and feel they add something extra to athletic contests. They are usually people who choose both opponents and circumstances that almost guarantee they will consistently win—or consistently lose, depending upon their ego needs. Any time the ego game becomes more important to you than the challenges of the objective game, you are going to find yourself in a double bind: it puts additional pressure on you to perform well and at the same time detracts from your ability to do so. If your mind is on whether the new tennis clothes you're wearing look okay, the chances are you'll miss a volley and feel you looked terrible doing it. If you think everyone's eyes are glued on you, it will keep your eyes from being glued to the ball. Self-consciousness distracts you from ball consciousness—and the ball, of course, doesn't care how you look. If sports is your way of expressing hostility, you may find anger ruining your timing, destroying finesse, and making a shambles of strategy. And the more caught up you are in your own ego games, the more easily you can be psyched out—distracted—by your opponent.

Psych-out games are employed all the time in sports. Some players try to psych their opponents deliberately. Others do it unconsciously, out of experience reinforced over the years of seeing other players fall apart in response to certain behavior. Veteran professional athletes often consciously utilize psych-outs, especially against younger players. Bill Russell gives a classic example of a psych-out he used when he was player-coach of the Boston Celtics. While in a restaurant he saw a player who was, he says, "younger and stronger than I was" and who he was going to face in a game the next day. Russell deliberately snubbed him. "I made sure he saw me, but I pretended not to recognize him. I didn't go over and say hello to him. I didn't even look at him the whole time I ordered, ate, and paid my check in full sight of him." The next day, Russell says, he had the player psyched. "He was out to get me, and I had him thinking about me instead of concentrating on the things he was supposed to do in the game. He was going to make me recognize him, show me who he was."

Most often, especially in recreational games, the psych-out takes the indirect approach of Russell's example, which can be deadly, because it gets to you without your recognizing it. However, sometimes the psych-out is less subtle. Muhammad Ali is famous for his vociferous taunting of opponents, both before and during his bouts. In tennis, Ilie Nastase has also been a frequent practitioner of this kind of psych-out. In one tournament match, in which he was trailing Ken Rosewall, he angrily disputed a call by a linesman and stormed off the court in mid-game, threatening to quit the match. An official finally talked him into returning. After this, Rosewall proceeded to lose eight straight games to Nastase and ultimately the match.

PSYCH-OUTS AS META-COMMUNICATION

"You are nobody; I am somebody."

The psych-out is conveyed by a process known in psychology as *meta-communication* ("meta" is from the Greek for "over" or "beyond"); it is something someone says to you through overall behavior, not directly in so many words. Although words may be employed, what's important is the message indicated beyond what is said. The meta-communication in Russell's example was: "You are nobody; I am somebody." In Ali it is "Even your best isn't good enough." Nastase's is "I'm the center of attention."

The insidious thing about meta-communication is that we receive it mainly on an emotional level rather than on an intellectual level where we could deal with it more rationally. If Russell's message was direct—if, for example, he had walked up to the other player and said, "You're nobody"—the other man might have been offended, but he would have been more likely to figure out that Russell was trying deliberately to provoke him. The meta-communication is apprehended unconsciously, and when its content is disturbing, it evokes a flash of emotions.

Psych-outs are *other-directed*. That is, they work because they get you to worrying about what other people think of you, rather than relying primarily on what you think of yourself. The more other-directed you tend to be, the more susceptible you are to psych-outs. On the other hand, the person who is trying to psych you out has to be other-directed, too, for he is demonstrating his insecurity by trying to rattle you. The person doing the psyching usually is very competitive and feels the need to use something extra to gain an edge in the game. When you notice a player trying to psych you out, it could be an indication that he is worried about your ability and thus vulnerable to psych-outs himself. And vulnerability to the turnabout naturally is greater in the person who is playing the ego game unconsciously and therefore unaware of his own weakness.

THE FOUR KINDS OF
PSYCH-OUT GAMES

Awareness is your greatest defense.

As we've stressed throughout the book, awareness is your prime defense against being psyched out and against slipping into unintentionally trying to psych out others. You may *want* to psych someone out, but at least you should be aware of what you are doing and also be cognizant of its pitfalls, the main one being that if you continually rely on trying to psych out other players you are admitting, "I'm not good enough to make it on my game alone."

Typically, psych-out games are of four kinds: they involve conscious or unconscious attempts at *provocation, intimidation, evoking guilt feelings,* or *distraction.* Here are common ones in each category.

1. Provocation

The Cold Shoulder. This is what Bill Russell was doing. It worked because he tapped into the yearning everyone has for some sort of recognition, this being especially pronounced among younger players looking up to veterans in big-time professional sports. It works best against anyone anxious to impress—newcomers to a club, novices at a game, employees playing bosses. It doesn't have to be as elaborate as Russell's scenario. The perpetrator simply feigns lack of interest in what the other player is doing, no matter how superb his performance may be. In effect, he turns his opponent into a backboard. The victim, for example, may sink a 25-foot putt and find it unnoticed. The meta-communication is: "Nothing you do interests or impresses me." Since the perpetrator never reacts to any "proof" of his opponent's skill, the victim keeps trying harder and harder for recognition and plays worse and worse.

Cage Rattling. Here the psych-out artist constantly taunts the victim, frequently under the guise of friendly kidding. It can be overt—for example, he says, "I hope you had your vitamins," or, "Is that the best you can do?" Or it can be subtle: "Did you manage to straighten out that slice since we last played?" The meta-communication is: "You don't scare me; even your best won't be good enough." The victim who falls for it is caught up in trying to prove otherwise, instead of concentrating on the game.

Teacher-Teacher. Here the psych-out artist gives the victim gratuitous lessons, correcting grip, stance, and the like—"You didn't flex your knees enough on that last shot; I used to have the same problem myself." The meta-communication is: "I'm the expert and you're the dumb-dumb." Another put-down in this category is faint praise: "That would have been a great shot if it had gone a little more to the right." Another such psych-out is condescension—this happens a lot between men and women, where the man tells the woman he'll "try to go easy" on her. Still another put-down is when the perpetrator goes out of the way to point out weaknesses in his opponent's game—for example, telling him to tee off when the next foursome is only 150 yards in front: "Go ahead and hit, Ralph, you'll never reach them." The meta-communication in all these cases is: "I'm superior; you're inferior."

2. Intimidation

Roaring Lion. The intimidating player likewise tries to impress his opponent with his superiority. In contact sports this often takes the form of extra hard hitting. A defensive front four in football, for example, will be sure to give the quarterback a good slam when they tackle him, or they'll tell him after the whistle blows, "We'll be back for you next play." Defensive tackle Otis Sistrunk of the Oakland Raiders says, for example, that the actual sack isn't as important as the intimidation. "Anything you're able to do to let that quarterback know you're breathing down his neck can spoil his play." In more subtle but equally intense games like tennis or golf the intimidation can take the form of showing a lot of razzle-dazzle during the warm-up period and discussing all the strong points of one's game with the victim. The meta-communication is: "Give up now; you don't have a chance."

Secret Weapon. Here the perpetrator points out some putative advantage over the opponent. He may, for example, let his victim know he has a new set of clubs or a new racquet, or has taken lessons, been to a clinic, practiced, or read the latest book on sports techniques (including this one) since they last met. The meta-communication is: "Now I've got you where I want you because of this new equipment. Your tools are surpassed." This kind of one-up-manship undoubtedly does a great deal to stimulate the sales of sports equipment. The new gear may not result in any lower scores, but it can often intimidate other players who haven't got the latest stuff.

3. Evoking Guilt Feelings

Always Mr. Nice Guy. This fellow tries to help and never fails to remind you what a terrific person and player you are. "Fantastic shot!" "Wow, I wish I could hit like you!" "I hope you don't mind playing with me." Mr. Nice may, in fact, be a sort of lovable chap. And he may actually enjoy the role of martyr and in this case have his own problem—that of setting too great a store in winning or losing and feeling he must lose in order to please others. But whether his act is a put-on or for real, you can be psyched out by it if you unconsciously take the behavior as a meta-communication that says: "You should be ashamed of yourself, trying to beat such a swell fellow like me." This type of player is also apt to spend a good deal of time apologizing for his errors. He I'm-sorry's his opponent to death. And when *you* start to apologize for your own good shots or lay back and not do your best, the psych has worked.

Poor Soul. This is the player who lets you know he's playing under a handicap. This can be communicated verbally—for example, "I haven't played since God knows when," or "Boy, do I have a hangover." The Poor Soul always has a sprained big toe, or has just been fired, or is going through a divorce. His communications can also be nonverbal; he may make a great show of some minor or even feigned injury—for example, showing up for the game wrapped in Ace bandages to elicit your sympathy. The meta-communication is: "You should be ashamed of picking on the handicapped. If you win, you're a rat. If I win, I'm a hero." But your feelings of guilt may be unwarranted. After all, it is your co-player's personal decision to play. If he's too debilitated, he shouldn't be out there. The key as to whether this is a psych-out ploy or not is in whether the complainer at the same time acts fiercely competitive in the game. There's nothing wrong with calling off competition and just playing an easy-going game if the other player isn't up to a tough contest. But when he begs for sympathy and then tries to beat the pants off you, it's most likely an attempted psych-out.

I Don't Care. This is a variation on Poor Soul. The perpetrator pretends not to care about competition. "I'm just out for the air," he says. "I'm not worried about who wins." His actions, however, contradict the words. You let down your guard and he proceeds to do everything in his power to trounce you. The meta-communication is: "If you win, it means nothing. If I win, it means I can whip you without even trying."

4. Distraction

Don't Look Now, but . . . Here the victim's concentration is diluted by all kinds of extraneous subject matter kindly provided by the psych-out artist. Golfers using this ploy may draw attention to all the perils of a particular course, all the traps, hazards, and roughs that wait for the ball. That way the victim is thinking more about what he shouldn't do than where he wants the ball to go. The meta-communication is: "Everything and everyone is out to get you. The other shoe will drop soon—on your head."

Temper Tantrums and Other Antics. Some players make this an integral part of their repertoire. They will clown around, talk to the ball, pray out loud for a great shot, give you a detailed analysis on what they did on the last play. They will complain loudly about every mishap, be it a bad bounce, a flub, or a close call by an official. It can be particularly telling in one-to-one games like tennis or handball. The meta-communication is: "I'm the center of attention; you're the foil. By paying attention to me it proves you are inferior."

Gee-Whizzing. One of the worst psych-outs is to make an opponent feel self-conscious. One weapon here is praise. It can either be of the innocuous "Gee, you're really hitting the ball today!" variety, or a snide reminder that the victim is playing a little "too well." The latter usually takes the form of friendly kidding. If you've just parred the last three holes in a golf game, the psych-out artist may then say, "Hey, I thought you said you were just a duffer. Are you going to par them all?" The meta-communication is: "You think you're big stuff, but we're watching you." It makes the victim start thinking consciously about what he has been doing and feel that continued superior performance now is expected, thus adding to the pressure. A variation is the innocent question that breaks the victim's concentration and stimulates too much conscious thought about technique—for example, "Do you breathe in or out during your serve?" If the victim starts thinking about that, it will be his fault.

AVOIDING PSYCH-OUT GAMES

The Sports Psyching techniques can help you.

The most effective way to psych out a psych-out artist is not to play any ego games at all, but to simply psych yourself *in* to your own game and play it the best you know how. If you are relaxed and concentrating and feel secure in your game, psych-outs are probably not going to rattle you. In fact, they probably will amuse you when you see other players trying them.

Psych-out attempts are almost always employed by players who are desperately eager to win. In professional sports, this is understandable, for the pressure to win comes down heavy—from the club owners, the fans, the athlete's family, the players themselves. But for recreational players, it's a lamentable bit of baggage that can ruin their game and the enjoyment of competition. There's a big difference between being a strong competitor and feeling that you must win at all costs.

Hopefully, also, the Sports Psyching techniques that you have learned will be so much a part of your own playing pattern that you will not have to resort to nonverbal psych-outs or be the instigator of verbal psyching of your opponent. If you find that you are communicating a great deal with your mouth instead of your sports equipment, the chances are that your own concentration is not what it should be.

Of course, not all communication on the playing field needs to be seen as a devious attempt by your opponent to disrupt your game. He may genuinely admire the way you are playing when he says, "Nice shot, champ!" He may really have a hangover when he claims to have one. And many players engage in psyching without really meaning to; as soon as they pick up their equipment, their months start to work, without their giving much thought to what's coming out. If you feel that this is the case with the people with whom you are playing, there is no reason why you cannot point out to them that their unconscious communication is not adding to your pleasure or theirs—or to their ability either.

Regardless of whether it's an intentional psych-out or not, however, the important point is your response to such things. It is your own game and your own responses to stimuli for which you must be responsible.

13

YOU AND YOUR INSTRUCTOR:
How to Get the Most Out of Those Expensive Lessons

There are tricks to learning just as there are to everything else.

You watch tennis matches on television and see some of your friends play. You think, "I'd like to play like that myself." You picture yourself playing, smashing serves into the corner, returning rallies down the line. Finally, you decide to take some lessons. You go to the Ace Tennis School. Your instructor may look like Robert Redford and seem able to put the ball anywhere he wants it to go. You think you detect a trace of boredom in his voice and manner as he gently rallies balls to you over the net. You miss most of them at first. You feel embarrassed. Eventually you start hitting them, but most go outside.

You're anxious to show him you are catching on, but as he goes over the fundamentals of the strokes with you, telling you to keep the racquet level through the ball, you are saying, "Yes, yes," only half listening, your mind impatiently anticipating the next session of rallying when you will have another chance to show him how well you can really hit the ball.

Every year millions of players take lessons, paying out millions of dollars, yet many really don't get that much out of them. "The biggest headache," says one golf instructor I know, "is that a lot of the people I get for lessons try to show me how well they can play instead of letting me see all the things they are doing wrong." Learning ability, then, is at least as important a part of building athletic performance as physical ability. Indeed, not learning part of your game properly can even lead to injuries. If you don't learn to get your body turning with your tennis stroke, for example, you are liable to swing with just your arm. You might get into this habit as a beginner, but as you learn to hit the ball harder, you place more strain on the muscles and tendons in your forearm connected to the elbow, causing little tears and bruises as they take the brunt of the impact transmitted from the racquet. And after a while, there you have it—tennis elbow.

It's hard to learn sports techniques totally on your own. You may pick up the details of a movement in instruction books, but you have no way, without someone watching you, to tell if you are, in fact, carrying them out right. Little mistakes creep in. When a weekend golfer has a chronic slice, the cause isn't that he lacks the strength or coordination to hit the ball straight. The reason is a faulty swing. He either didn't learn it correctly in the first place or he has unwittingly slipped into habitually incorrect motions. In other words, he forgot what he learned.

Sometimes just being able to at least hit the ball is enough of a reward for a beginner to reinforce a bad habit. Indeed, the wrong move even begins to *feel* right, and when that happens your game becomes fixed at a specific level because your flawed technique can carry you only so far.

Even if you are an experienced player, it is possible to unconsciously fall into the habit of errors. The best athletes insure themselves against this by having continual coaching.

Jack Nicklaus says that he returns to his teacher, Jack Grout, each year. "We begin at the beginning with grip and setup and go right through the fundamentals," he says. "There isn't a golfer in the world who wouldn't benefit from a similar periodic checkup."

Most weekend athletes, however, don't have the time or money for such intensive instruction. For most, it is a sporadic effort at best: a short series of lessons for the beginner, perhaps a week's vacation-clinic for the experienced player. It is doubly important, therefore, for the recreational athlete to get the most from those expensive lessons. Unfortunately, he usually gets a lot less—and the reason often is that there are all kinds of emotional-psychological problems that crop up which interfere with the learning process.

PSYCHOLOGICAL BARRIERS BETWEEN STUDENT AND TEACHER

The mistake of trying to avoid mistakes.

Taking lessons is not a mechanical process whereby you go to a teacher and he gives you the knowledge and you take it away with you and practice, and so on. It involves the interaction of human beings, fraught with all the problems that this implies. It is also burdened with the social myths that, as we discussed earlier in the book, most of us carry into athletics. Much of my work over the years has been in exploring the relationships of coaches and players and trying to help them work together more effectively. During that time I have observed four patterns of behavior which complicate things.

1. The myth of athletic prowess. Many weekend athletes go to an instructor unconsciously expecting to be molded into the fantasies they have about being an outstanding player. They picture themselves as ready to give all in this noble effort to become a superlative competitor. To think that it will result in anything less would not be "the right attitude." At today's prices they probably have a reason to feel that way, but, realistically, they not only are setting themselves up for disappointment, they are creating a difficult situation from the first lesson onward. It immediately puts pressure on both the student and instructor.

2. The feeling of inadequacy. Students bring a certain degree of timidity into the relationship with the instructor. They look up to the instructor and, again unconsciously reflecting the you-gotta-be-a-hero folklore, feel vulnerable and embarrassed about not already being as good as the teacher. Such feelings of inadequacy cause reactions that often get in the way of learning—for example, making you act defensively rather than being open to advice, making you say, in effect, "I'm sorry I don't know as much as I should."

3. Discomfort in the student role. Many adults feel uncomfortable in the student role. They don't have much to relate to it except their experiences as children in school and may resent being cast into what they feel is a similar role. Moreover, the weekend athlete taking private lessons often comes from a different socioeconomic bracket than the instructor. The student might be a successful executive or professional and feel awkward in the role of a neophyte sitting at the feet of the teacher.

4. Anxiety at being judged. Whether you know it or not, you may feel that the instructor is judging you rather than making an assessment of your game. Of course, he is supposed to do the latter; checking over flaws in your technique is part of the job. But if you feel that this is a judgment of you as a person—if it brings up all those anxious feelings which you associate with how well you used to do in high school gym class, of whether you are "good" or "bad"—this will quite naturally lead to your setting up psychological defenses that will inhibit your ability to learn from the lessons.

What are the common reactions to all these insecurities?

You may react by apologizing for missing shots. A tennis instructor I worked with once remarked that some of his students said "I'm sorry" almost as often as they tried to hit the ball.

You may showboat. You may go to an instructor to correct flaws in your game but end up hiding them by trying instead to show your best stuff.

You may be too quick to indicate that you have caught on to something and not ask clarifying questions for fear of appearing slow.

You may follow the instructor's directions to the letter, without really digesting them and without experimenting with the coach's advice in order to get the feel of things for yourself. (This dependency is also a defense mechanism: if things don't go right, then you can blame the instructor because, after all, you did everything you were told to do.)

What all this adds up to is *the fear of making mistakes.* Who can blame any of us? After all, not only our athletic instruction but most of our schooling emphasizes getting the right answers. As students in school we learn to anticipate the responses the teacher will want and to avoid errors at all costs. So, most of us are conditioned to overlook the value of making mistakes in trying to learn anything. And there is no area where this is more true than in sports. The idea that you can find out more about your golf swing by slicing than by making a nice but not so terrific straight shot is alien to our thinking. But it is true. If you are too afraid of flubbing, you will approach your lessons too conservatively to learn. Your thinking will be rigid.

Tennis teacher Vic Braden says fear of being in the wrong is the most common learning obstacle he notes in his pupils. He counters this tendency by telling them that his famous College of Tennis in Cote de Caza, California, is a "mistake center."

"I try to set up a system where they are rewarded for finding mistakes in their techniques and correcting them and then going on to find more mistakes," he says. "I tell them to try things out for themselves. If they are standing too close to the net, I encourage them to exaggerate the correction, even if they miss the ball by doing this at first. That way they discover the right distance for themselves."

FAILURE AS A SELF-FULFILLING PROPHECY

The defense against mistakes can make you overestimate your limitations.

Avoiding exposing yourself and making mistakes can lead you into the position of feeling you can't do it. The golfer with the chronic slice certainly has the ability to avoid that slice. He can say, "Yes, if I find out what's wrong and change my swing, I can hit a straight ball." But instead he may go the opposite direction and say, "I'll never hit the ball straight; I'm no good." How many times have you heard other players say, "I'll never get it. It's hopeless"?

The problem is a lack of confidence, which becomes a defense against having to try, thus avoiding risk of failure. Braden says that a common statement from his beginning pupils is "I'm uncoordinated," thus apologizing for failure

in advance and so signaling him not to expect anything—
even though there is nothing wrong with their coordination.
("I tell them not to worry about it," Braden says. "If they
can walk to the drinking fountain without falling down,
they are okay. They have a play right there.") Making such
statements continually can mess up your chances of improving your game. If you think yourself uncoordinated,
you increase the chances you will *act* uncoordinated. Every
clumsy act will reinforce the notion and take your attention
off any instructions that might help you play better. Every
time you can't carry out the instructions—which for beginners will be *most* of the time—it will be an excuse for lack
of progress, a self-fulfilling prophecy ("See? I told you I was
uncoordinated") that leads to eventual despair.

How do we change all this?

PICKING THE RIGHT TEACHER

*How to achieve the most important goal—satisfying
yourself.*

The principal thing to realize about sports instruction is
this: You are not doing it for the coach or anyone else; you
are doing it for yourself. You are the one who is paying the
fees, and you will live with your game long after you and
your teacher have parted company. Thus, you should take
some care about picking the instructor and type of lessons
best suited to you. This will help reinforce the idea that
you, not your instructor, are the center of the action.

There are several points to consider in picking an instructor:

Do you want group or individual lessons? Some people
don't learn well in a group situation. They feel self-
conscious around other people. They start to feel competitive with other members of the group, gauging their progress

against that of the others rather than concentrating on their own development. On the other hand, group lessons are usually cheaper (except for clinics, tennis ranches, and the like), and the group can provide support and a degree of anonymity.

As far as clinics, camps, and schools go, check whether someone is there who shows some definite concern. Many carry the name of a famous athlete who makes at best only a guest appearance. (Sometimes this is for the best because not every great player is a great teacher.) But even if the person isn't actually there, it still could be a good school or clinic, provided that the person really in charge is running a good program. Talk over the program with him to see how well it is run.

Here are the questions to ask: Do they have a time schedule that breaks down each aspect of the game? Does the program include time for practice and checks on your progress as well as the passing out of information? Is there time for individual instruction as well as the group activities? What is the student-teacher ratio? There is no single right answer to these questions; however, the answers can help you make comparisons to see which school seems right for you.

Beyond these very basic requirements you should check to see how enjoyable the instructions make the learning experience. Some people believe one has to suffer under Prussian-like discipline to learn anything. But unless your level of competition demands it (you are training for the Olympics, say), two weeks of Spartan training is not going to do your game much good. On the contrary, the more supportive and enjoyable the experience is, the better chance you'll have of forming positive habits out of the skills you'll be learning. So you should ask about the school's general approach, making sure you get what you need from it.

Certainly when you are taking individual lessons and paying $10 to $30 for an hour, you've a right to be choosy. You should expect a teacher to go beyond just mechanically recognizing physical performance problems. He should pay some attention to your psychological needs. This doesn't mean stretching you out on a couch and rummaging through your childhood memories. It just means he should have the sensitivity to discern whether you tend to tighten up, are impatient to progress too fast, tend to drive yourself too hard, or lack self-confidence, and to be able to adapt his teaching approach to your emotional responses.

This isn't as complicated as it first seems. For example, suppose you are taking a golf lesson and you have skulled the ball several times with your 5-iron. Each time you do it you feel more self-conscious, so you unconsciously adjust by chopping harder at the ball, producing an even worse shot. A less astute pro might simply tell you drily that you are chopping at the ball and that you should slow down your backswing. A more perceptive teacher might tell you to stop for a moment, ease up, loosen your grip on your club, and take some practice swings slowly without hitting the ball; then, when he sees you are relaxed and have the swing under control, he would tell you to step up to the ball again.

If you are going to invest in a series of lessons with one instructor, it is advisable to get permission to watch a lesson or two before you sign up, to see whether you think you will have rapport with him. Then once you have settled on the teacher, you should place yourself in his hands and follow his instructions. This relationship doesn't mean slavish devotion; it should operate on the assumption that you and your teacher are partners having the same goal—namely, to improve your skills. Thus, the last thing you want is to be defensive. To improve student-instructor rapport and enhance the learning situation, I have designed a questionnaire *(see next page)*.

QUESTIONNAIRE REGARDING STUDENT'S REACTION TO INSTRUCTION

Listed below are a brief series of statements reflecting the student's reactions to instruction. The student should check the appropriate column as it relates to him.

The point of this questionnaire is to help instructors and

STUDENT'S REACTION TO INSTRUCTOR

1. I feel personally judged by my instructor.
2. I'm afraid of "looking bad" when performing in front of my instructor.
3. I've done things to please my instructor rather than myself.
4. I apologize when I make an error.
5. I try to show off to impress the instructor.
6. I hide things my instructor should know, which would embarrass me if he found out.
7. I do not ask for clarification if I do not understand something.
8. I concentrate on *how* my instructor says something rather than *what* he says.
9. I do only what the instructor says because I'm afraid of what he'll say.
10. I make excuses for doing poorly.
11. I've exaggerated my exploits on and/or off the field to impress my instructor.
12. I am secretly afraid of my instructor.

students overcome their usual inhibitions about discussing how they view each other and to get them communicating on the same wavelength. Indeed, it may be worthwhile giving up one lesson to go over this material since it is bound to enhance the effectiveness of the rest of the lessons.

	ALMOST ALWAYS	OFTEN	SOME- TIMES	SELDOM	ALMOST NEVER
1.	_____	_____	_____	_____	_____
2.	_____	_____	_____	_____	_____
3.	_____	_____	_____	_____	_____
4.	_____	_____	_____	_____	_____
5.	_____	_____	_____	_____	_____
6.	_____	_____	_____	_____	_____
7.	_____	_____	_____	_____	_____
8.	_____	_____	_____	_____	_____
9.	_____	_____	_____	_____	_____
10.	_____	_____	_____	_____	_____
11.	_____	_____	_____	_____	_____
12.	_____	_____	_____	_____	_____

THEY'RE YOUR LESSONS

Making the instructions work for you.

No matter how knowledgeable, communicative, perceptive, and inspiring your instructor, the main job of
making the lessons work is yours. The instructor can give
you information, guide you, and correct you, but in the end
it is you who must digest the lessons and assimilate them
into your own behavior. The teacher can tell you how to
swing a golf club, watch you try it, and correct your
motions, but you have to understand and feel how to do it
correctly from inside yourself in order to remember how to
reproduce it on the golf course.

I will not give you a lecture here about the necessity for
hard work. Sure, plenty of practice isn't going to hurt, but,
really, how many hours do you have to devote to it? You
want to use the time you do have to its greatest advantage.
Diligence and lessons won't ensure improved performance,
any more than will the most expensive equipment. The
important thing is *how* you take the lessons rather than in
how much money or time you spend.

The skills you learn in sports are physical as well as
mental. It's no good just to know how you should move,
you must be able to make the proper movement, without
having to stop and think about it. Your body as well as your
mind has to know what to do. The trouble with sports
instruction is that, even though we look at pictures and
diagrams and watch others perform, most of it is transmitted to us in the form of words. Teachers and instruction
books give us directions, which we must then translate into
the language of our own movements. We must make the
jump from words to actions—and most of the time, unfortunately, it is done unconsciously and haphazardly: we keep

plugging at our lessons and practice and hope it will some-how sink in.

However, it doesn't have to be that hit-or-miss.

WHAT TO DO BEFORE, DURING, AND AFTER THE LESSONS

Going from learning to doing.

In counseling I have found there are steps anyone can take that will help turn instruction into fully assimilated knowledge, that will take you from learning about a skill to actually acquiring it. This means, first, you must set aside the emotional barriers of the student-teacher relationship so you can concentrate on the lesson.

What to Do Before the Lessons

Set realistic goals. Lessons shouldn't be approached with open-ended expectations. That only sets you up for dis-appointment. If you are getting intermediate or advanced lessons in a game you already play, pinpoint with your instructor just what you need to improve. If you want, tell him what you *think* is wrong with your game; but, re-member, his assessment is the key. Then, once you agree on what needs work, commit yourself totally to that program.

Prepare yourself mentally. A good time for this is when you are getting into the clothes you will wear for your lesson. Many athletes I know make dressing for a game or for the lesson part of a ritual. It is a good time to go over in your mind what you will try to accomplish in the forth-coming session. Your mood is important. You want to feel relaxed and receptive. In many ways you can use your sports clothes as if they were a team uniform. Simply by putting them on should help create an appropriate mood.

Arrive early for your lesson. Perhaps you can watch someone else taking a lesson ahead of you. Take some time to think more about what you want to try for during this lesson. If possible, arrange to have your lesson at a time and place where you feel comfortable. Some people function better in the morning, others later in the day. If all this sounds self-centered, that's exactly what's intended. The purpose of the lessons, after all, is to improve *your* game.

What to Do During the Lessons

Don't rush. In a half-hour lesson you should concentrate on getting down only one or two plays rather than rushing through many. The worst enemy to learning is the tendency to hurry. Too anxious to show what we have learned, we hastily try to put the information into action—and the result is that it slips away from us.

Don't reject your errors. The wrong move generally feels wrong, and although you never want to practice an error, remembering how it felt can be a clue in the future to correcting a problem in your game. Learn from your mistakes, but don't consciously repeat them.

Don't try harder. Consciously telling yourself to try harder, to do better, rather than getting more deeply into the flow of your action through relaxed concentration, is not productive. What the instructor is telling you isn't a command (against which you may unconsciously rebel); it is an invitation to allow yourself to do the act correctly.

Ask questions. Don't let anything slip by you that is unclear. Check out details of what the instructor tells you. Repeat instructions back: "Let's see, I put my feet here, weight balanced this way, turn the body, arms, cock the wrist, arc in this direction . . ." and so forth.

Watch carefully. Don't rely solely on verbal instructions. Make sure the instructor shows you how a play should be executed so that you have a clear picture of it. Concentrate on what you are seeing and hearing, just as you have learned to concentrate on the here and now during a game. Have him show you again and again. The eye-brain connection is as important as the one from the ear to the brain. Videotape on closed-circuit TV, used by many sports instruction schools, is valuable as a diagnostic device and later as a way of getting feedback on progress, but it doesn't replace a good instructor. The TV can show you if you are doing something wrong, but only the instructor can show you how to fix it. (TV can also get you worried about how you look. Most people are so used to seeing the strong, good-looking athletes on TV that they almost can't bear to look at themselves.)

Get the feel of it. Ask the instructor for tips on how it should feel, in terms of balance, muscle tension, timing. Every time you are successful in carrying out a play, make a mental note of how it felt. What you are doing, in this way, is building up both mental and muscle memory of the action. Experiment with variations of the motions, even to the point of exaggeration. What you want to do is *tune in* the feelings of the play action until you get it down most effectively for your musculature. It's like tuning in a radio station until you have the strongest signal.

Couple the learned motions with key phrases. An instructor can usually give you several of these phrases—a golf pro, for example, will tell you to "let the clubhead go through the ball." Then you can link the phrase "through the ball" to the effortless feeling—when you have hit the ball correctly—of the clubhead connecting and following through. This linking of proper motions and key phrases should be made for all segments of a play. Later you will be able to use this to rehearse the play in your mind, remembering the motions and feelings automatically as you recite the list of phrases that make up the play.

What to Do After the Lessons and in Play

Review the lesson. Learning should not end when the lesson is over. Think about each portion of the game on which you worked—verbally, visually, and physically. If you can, make short, specific notes that can cue you later into the essence of your new learning. Think about what the instructor told you, how each play looked, how the motions felt. There is a natural tendency for everyone to mentally replay the good shots in any game. Take advantage of this after the lesson and run your own imaginary videotape of each occasion you succeeded in carrying out instructions.

Keep your expectations in check. Learning isn't automatic. Don't expect that you'll be able to use your new skill perfectly right away. In fact, sometimes you can expect to get worse before you get better, especially if you are an experienced player trying to correct faulty habits, since the faulty habit will still feel right. Reverting to old ways is easy, staying with the new is hard. Take practice time both between the lessons and after a series of lessons is completed. Practice the new material in nonthreatening, non-competitive situations at first, until you are ready to use it in competitive play.

Work with the new technique. It's like a two-finger hunt-and-peck typist who could do forty words a minute with two fingers learning to touch-type with all ten fingers and thereby doubling the typing speed. Learning, for everyone, involves struggle and moments of disappointment. It isn't easy, so it's important to weigh your priorities.

How much do you really wish to improve performance skills and how much are you willing to pay for it in terms of time and effort? You might answer that by saying, "Well, basically I'm happy with my game" and leave it at that. Or you may enjoy setting a challenge for yourself and using lessons to work toward it. The important thing is that it's *your* challenge, not set by someone else or some athletic hero myth. Make it for you and by you.

WINNING: 14
What It Is and What It Isn't

Behind it all is the fear of coming in last.

It may seem that the whole point of this book is to show you how to win.

It is not.

The idea (attributed to Vince Lombardi) that winning isn't everything, that it's the only thing, is the shibboleth of sports. It makes sports nothing more than a continuing struggle to maintain a pecking order. It means nothing if the game is done just for itself, for the fun or the pride of doing it well; the only satisfaction is of prevailing over someone else, and the only motivation for playing is to be number one. While the "winning is everything" view creates a dramatic life and death struggle that helps sell stadium tickets (although, conversely, it can also make sports less interesting to watch—witness the dulling effects of ball-control offense or zone defense, which prompted some NFL rule changes to liven things up), as far as sports *participation* is concerned, it is just one more ego game, an extra layer of emotional self-investment that has nothing to do with the objective part of any sport. There is nothing wrong with competition, or of giving your best in competition, but the idea that winning is the *only* thing—that the final score is the be-all and end-all—makes it harder for a player to reach his full potential, to play his best game.

Even professional athletes generally try to leave desperate thoughts of "winning is everything" out of mind when the game begins. They want to be "up" for a game but not paralyzed by exaggerated notions of the importance of winning. Byron Nelson, for example, said that when this "must win" attitude started to flood his mind during a major golf tournament, he would reduce tension by imagining the worst that could happen—namely, that he could come in last. Then he would think, "So what?" He would accept that as not such a horrible fate, and this would help him to relax, concentrate on the action, and perform better.

The professional player, of course, has some real basis for concern. After all, he has invested years in sports as a career. Sports is the pro's business, and losing is bad for business. For the recreational player, however, sports often is trying to get away from worries about business. But instead of gaining a few hours away from the rat race, he finds he's created his own rat race.

Winning is, of course, more fun than losing, and the desire to win is nothing to be ashamed of. But when the desire to win becomes the sole source of gratification from a sport, then we are as impoverished as if the sole value in food was its taste and not the nutrition we also receive.

DOES WINNING MEAN EXCELLENCE?

The score is not the final count.

Who wins the "winning is everything" derby? Not you. If you compete with players of ability equal to yours, you are setting yourself up for disappointment about 50 percent of the time. If you compete with players who are more capable than yourself, you set yourself up for an even greater percentage of unsatisfactory games. If you seek out less skilled competitors, you could win all the time, but you wouldn't feel like a winner. The only players who win the winning-is-everything game, really, are the handful who end up as superchampions in sports. Everyone else has been or can be beaten by someone else who is one rung above them on the ladder.

Winning athletic contests, moreover, is not all it's cracked up to be even in terms of measuring quality of performance. There are lots of ways to win a game, not all of them involving skill. You can be lucky. Your opponent can be having an off day. We exaggerate the assertive factor in sports victories. Indeed most recreational athletics is won on the other person's mistakes as often as on one's own feats. Sportscasters talk about the "superior push" of the winning team, when they might well be summing up the penalties and fumbles that led to a football defeat. As Vic Braden put it, "We like to think that we can go out there and push people around, just blow them off the court. But what really happens is you beat yourself or the other guy loses to you."

Part of the problem is in how winners are determined. Winning, in the conventional sense, means making a better score. But the score is only one kind of measurement of the game, and it's a pretty thin substitute for the actual experience of playing. You spend hours playing and all you have to show for it is a bunch of little numbers on a piece of paper—or maybe just in your head—and this, furthermore, is supposed to be the only thing that matters. Overemphasis on who piles up more points is a narrow view of athletic accomplishment. As philosopher John McMurty, of Canada's Guelph University, told a sports symposium: "The pursuit of victory works to reduce the chance for excellence in the true performance by rendering it subservient to emerging victorious. I suspect that our conventional mistake of presuming the opposite—presuming that the contest-for-prize framework and excellence of performance are somehow related as a unique cause and effect—may be the deepest-lying prejudice of civilized thought. Keeping score in any game—especially team games—is a substantial indication that the activity in question is not interesting enough in itself to those who keep score."

THE SCORE ABOUT THE SCORE

What it doesn't show.

In most athletics the scorecard is too rigid to allow points for all sorts of things that figure into the quality of your game. Except for sports such as diving and figure skating, you don't get points for having a great style, or making a particularly beautiful play, or doing something you've been trying for months, or playing an inspired second half even though poor performance in the first half cost you the game. You don't get points for having a lot of fun. You don't get points for these important things.

As anyone knows, you can play poorly and win, or perform well and lose. The score reflects a lot of other factors and depends on *who* you play. If you, as an amateur, recreational player, somehow had a tennis match with Chris Evert or John Newcombe, your friends wouldn't ask who won. They might ask *how* you played and your answer could be that you played one of your best, most memorable, and most fulfilling games, even though you lost the match.

It's common for us to play over our heads against superior opposition, because this foreknowledge that winning is not an essential part of the experience is what brings out our best performances. You know that against a pro you'd have no chance of prevailing and so, giving up that idea, you might focus on doing your best with each shot. The superior player gives you superior opposition against which to pit your abilities, play by play. If you are not intimidated by the idea of losing (a foregone conclusion) or "looking bad," you can simply concentrate on playing and sometimes go beyond yourself.

This experience of playing over your head, doing something you didn't think you could do, is one of the greatest rewards of athletics. It's the basic challenge of all sports. From it we derive magic moments as participants. They provide what some humanistic psychologists (such as the late Abraham Maslow) have called *peak experiences*—remarkable moments in our lives when our behavior transcends the mundane, everyday routine, when we feel as if we are doing everything correctly, as if our behavior were without a flaw.

George Plimpton, in *Paper Lion*, *The Bogey Man*, and other books, showed us you don't have to be a winner to be a hero. We admired him just for going in there against such overwhelming competition with professional superstars, for somehow keeping his dignity and wry sense of humor, all the while recognizing how inept he must have looked. The excitement and the experience were what was important in the end. It is Plimpton's recognition of human foibles and human values that lie beyond the spectator sports hoopla that makes his writings so compelling.

Nowadays we tend to snicker at the Grantland Rice verse:

When the One Great Scorer comes to write against your name
He marks—not if you won or lost—but how you played the game.

But corny as it may sound, this does represent the original ideals of athletics far better than "winning is everything." This was the intent of the Olympics—not pseudo-warfare among nations, Communist vs. non-Communist, Third World vs. industrial countries, and so on, but a celebration of the miraculous and beautiful things of which the human body is capable. Perhaps in twenty or thirty years we'll snicker just as much at the "winning is everything" slogan.

COOPERATION GAMES

Putting competition in perspective.

In many games—golf or bowling, for example—your co-players aren't even the primary source of opposition. It is the physical characteristics of the game that present the obstacles you try to overcome. You try to get around the eighteen holes in a minimum number of strokes; you try to bowl over as many pins as you can in ten frames. You and your co-players strive toward an ideal goal—it's *both* of you against the physical challenges of the game—and at the end of play the one who came close to that goal is the winner.

Even games of direct interplay, like tennis or handball, don't *require* an attitude of confrontation. You can perform just as well or better with the idea that you and your opponent really are cooperating to make good games for each other. Timothy Gallwey, in *The Inner Game of Tennis*, explains the logic this way:

> Winning is overcoming obstacles to reach a goal. . . . Once one recognizes the value of having difficult obstacles to overcome, it is a simple matter to see the true benefit that can be gained from competitive sports. In tennis, who is it that provides a person with the obstacles he needs in order to experience

his highest limits? His opponent, of course! Then is your opponent a friend or an enemy? He is a friend to the extent that he does his best to make things difficult for you. Only by competing does he in fact cooperate. So we arrive at the startling conclusion that true competition is identical with true cooperation.

The tennis opponent, if looked at in this way, then becomes analogous to a golf course architect, who does his diabolical best to make the fairways fearsomely interesting. If you score higher than your usual average on a difficult golf course, you wouldn't ordinarily feel that you were humiliated by the golf course architect. Neither would you feel that you were one-up on the architect if your score were low.

We are so used to looking at sports in the context of competition that we often confuse competitiveness with the whole experience. Again, our fascination with spectator sports bolsters this prejudice. The Trojans play the Irish, and we ask "Who won?"—not "What happened?" And you ask yourself the same question—who won rather than what happened—when you go bowling with your neighbor. What one should do after every game, when he asks himself "How did I do?" is to answer not "I won or I lost," but say, "I enjoyed myself, especially the moment when such-and-such happened and the way this or that felt." The ego game of one-upmanship that we attach to athletics can be eliminated—and yet we can still have all the elements of sports, all the challenges, the satisfaction of overcoming obstacles, the possibilities for physical and skill development, the enjoyment.

Let's say that you changed the rules of tennis to eliminate competition and substituted cooperation. In the new game of Cooperation Tennis, the object would be for you and your partner to keep the ball in motion back and forth across the net, landing each time in bounds. Let's say that, to make it interesting, the ball would have to land in a different part of the court each time and that you'd have to alternate types of strokes—forehand, backhand, overheads, lobs, and so on—never hitting two successive shots with the same kind of stroke. You could play Cooperation Tennis for endurance—that is, to see how many you could hit back and forth without a mistake in sequence or hitting it out or hitting the net. You could also play Cooperation Tennis for speed—to see how many rallies you could make in a fixed time, say one minute. Anyone walking by your court would be hard put to tell you weren't playing conventional tennis.

Cooperation Tennis would have much the same kind of action as ordinary tennis. It could be just as exciting, as you and your partner endeavor to keep the ball in play. It would require skill in the various kinds of shots and in placing the ball. There would be dramatic moments when some of your shots inevitably would be near misses, hitting close to the line, followed by thrilling play-making as your partner saved the shot and kept the game going.

Some bright fellow might come along and say, "Hey, this would make a big hit as a spectator sport. We could form teams of top tennis players. They could compete against each other, with each team being scored not only on numbers of rallies, but on the precision and style of their shot combinations, rather like gymnasts or figure skaters are judged. We could put it on television." You'd then be back to competition, and this could be fun, too, as long as everyone who played the new version of the game didn't revert to anxiety games over which team was number one. The point is that the competitive aspect of Cooperation Tennis would be something that was *added* later and of no consequence in relation to the basic values of the game. If players wanted to do it that way, fine, but you also could get along just fine without it.

A friend of mine and his friend decided that they would revise the rules of tennis to fit their goals. Both of them were average players, and like most average players their second serve did little more than get the ball into play. Neither of them were happy with the situation because whether they won or lost the point on the second serve, they felt like losers. The server knew that by just getting the ball into the receiving court, he was not serving the way he should. If the receiver put the ball away, the server felt appropriately punished for the weak serve, but if the receiver netted the ball, the server didn't feel that he had really won the point. On the other side of the net, the receiver didn't feel any sense of accomplishment by putting away a weak serve and if he put the ball into the net or hit it out, he felt "I can't even handle the easy ones." They solved this no-win proposition by deciding to take as many as four serves but making sure that each one was a hard "first" serve. Not only did they very quickly find that the quality of their serves improved because of the practice, but that the quality of the whole game improved because they were hitting out fully, not only on the serve, but during the rallying as well.

You could revise the rules of other games as well, to bring cooperation overtly into them. In Cooperation Golf, for example, you and your partner would alternately hit each other's shots. You would tee off, then your partner would hit your ball (call it Ball A) from where it landed on the fairway. You would, in turn, hit your partner's ball (call it Ball B) after he hit it off the tee, each of you would alternate right up to the final putts. The goal would be how few shots you and your partner—and this time *really* your partner—could take in a round. You could use the same alternating shot system to play Cooperation Bowling.

Stewart Brand (a creator of *The Whole Earth Catalog*) invented a number of games for what eventually became the

New Games Foundation in Marin County north of San Francisco. These games have been played by thousands at New Games Festivals first in the San Francisco Bay area in the early 1970s and then elsewhere. The games stress mass participation rather than specialization and performance as do traditional sports games. The motto is "Play hard! Play fair! Nobody hurt!" Competition is deemphasized. In games like Earth Ball, for example, the idea is for a number of people to keep a huge inflated ball aloft for as long as possible. Similarly, in Infinity Volleyball the object is to just keep the ball going. The New Games Foundation people have started programs in schools across the country and believe that one day their games will be equal to if not replace games like football and baseball in popularity because they reflect better the values we desire in our society.

If you are a person who enjoys strenuous competition, you might not want to play cooperation sports. But if you've found the pressures of rivalry spoiling your enjoyment of sports because, like most of us, you've been conditioned to lay too much importance on them, then you might want to try a cooperation game, or make one up. It's a good object lesson in putting competition in its proper perspective.

THE RECREATIONAL
ATHLETE'S CONTRACT

The real definition of a winner.

"Winning isn't everything," George Leonard says, "it isn't *anything*." The author of *The Ultimate Athlete* and cofounder of the Esalen Sports Center, Leonard isn't against competition, only its overemphasis. "Competition is the spice of sports," he says, "but if you make spice the whole meal, you'll be sick "

What is needed is a concept of winning that goes beyond trophies. In *What Do You Say After You Say Hello?* Dr. Eric Berne defines a winner as "a person who fulfills his contract with the world and with himself. That is, he sets out to do something, says that he is committed to doing it, and in the long run does it." He points out that it doesn't matter what the goal of the contract happens to be, as long as the person sets it for himself.

What we are advocating in this book is the rewarding of the *process* of participation for personal goals, needs, or values—not the *scored* product of the participation. To do this you must develop a contract with yourself in which you determine what you wish to get out of your participation, your personal reasons for playing a game. Then reward yourself every time you try, as you take each small step toward the goal. The ideal contract you should make with yourself is for a dual payoff: (1) "If I make it, wonderful." (2) "If I don't make it, I give myself credit for the attempt." You don't have to look beyond the experience of the game itself to obtain all the benefits—psychological, physical, and social—that can accrue from athletics. No matter what your level of performance is, you can become a champion in the full enjoyment of your game

Afterword

GROW WITH YOUR GAME:
Using Sports to Help Your Life

I've had my say about Sports Psyching, but while I have your attention I'd like to add a few words about how you may relate the techniques and awareness you have gained to a larger arena—life psyching.

On a conscious level we tend to put sports off in a corner as if it were a spare part left over when our lives were assembled. But sports *does* have a connection with our lives—a fundamental one. Your game brings out characteristic behavior more vividly than does ordinary experience. Almost like a laboratory, it isolates and magnifies your typical reactions. What's more, as the pressures of any game become greater, your more deep-seated personal characteristics become apparent. If we can change the impediments of the joy of sports, perhaps we can do the same for other aspects of our lives.

The more obvious emotional reactions you experience under pressure in sports can give you insights to some tendencies you have in reacting to the generally more subtle and complex pressures of life. It can set off in bold relief some otherwise obscure outlines of how you feel about yourself and the world when faced with challenge and risk.

The more pressure you feel in a game, the more such characteristics show themselves. Even the *kinds* of pressure you experience can demonstrate some of your inner attitudes and proclivities, for you choose your particular pressure according to the kind of person you are. For example, the highly competitive person feels a compulsion to win at almost any cost. Another type of person may feel a need to play the role of a loser in order to please friends who are more competitive. Sometimes reaction to pressure in sports can even indicate a certain degree of pathology, not necessarily mental disturbance, but a tendency toward certain neurotic syndromes. Any personally unproductive behavior— i.e., depression, obsessive thinking about missed shots, or thought about "revenge" that last for days after a contest— would be classified in that category.

Just as you have learned to be more objectively critical and less condemnatory about your game, so you should apply the same principles to your life. Experience can become your teacher, not a source of negative judgments. Breaking down your problems in your game is little different from breaking down the problems in your life—the process always ends up leaving you with a more manageable view of your difficulties and the ability to set reasonable goals. Depending on his personality, everyone tends to experience some degree of anxiety when facing self-chosen challenges like examinations, interviews, meetings with clients, public speaking engagements, or any one of a hundred stress-producing circumstances. These are pressure situations that are analogous to sports because you choose to put yourself into them. And they are susceptible to the Sports Psyching approach because your object is to weed out extraneous anxiety and control yourself in the situation.

A certain degree of anxiety is productive and probably unavoidable. But, just as in sports, there are times when the anxiety levels can interfere with performance and keep you from achieving your potential. If this tends to happen to you, the first thing to do is to find out how and why such anxieties occur, so you can deal with them before any emotional snowballing takes place. The Sports Emotional-Reaction Profile in Chapters 5 and 6 can give you pointers; correlating your personality traits with the kinds of pressures that tend to affect you on the playing field can lead to greater self-awareness about your reactions to stress situations off the field, too.

The way to ascertain the pattern of your pressure responses is to monitor your thoughts and feelings before, during, and after a game.

How do you feel *before* the start of a game? What do you expect? Do you usually think you will win or lose? Do you avoid thinking about the game altogether? What is your worst fear—that you will look bad, that you will fail to live up to your own expectations or your opponents, perhaps even that other players will dislike you for succeeding—or failing?

What are your reactions *during* the game. What do you feel when you make a good play? Does it make you feel superior? Does it make you feel like the *next* play should be just as good or better? Do you praise yourself? Do you feel embarrassed at outdoing other players? How do you react after flubbing an easy shot? Depressed? Panicky? Are you quickly able to spot what caused the trouble and move on to the next play, or do you feel guilty or angry with yourself? Do you blame outside influences?

How do you react *after* a game? When you lose, do you try to hide? Do you want to leave without talking to anyone? Are you angry with yourself? When you *win* do you feel superior to other players? Do you like to rub it in? Do you feel embarrassed and alibi your success?

As you think about the answers to these questions within

the framework of your sports experience, you might well be able to see how such behavior connects up with your responses to the challenges and stresses of daily life. Having learned how to isolate and handle them on the athletic field, you can now think about isolating and handling them off the field.

Listen to yourself during the game. Frequently, the things you will hear yourself saying are immensely revealing. For example, if you find yourself saying "I'll never get it right," I can assure you that you are not making an objective judgment related to the immediate challenge; you may simply be repeating long-forgotten criticism in childhood by a parental figure who would ask, "Can't you do anything right?" When you mumble your own name out on the playing field, much as an angry parent might, you are reliving a past which can destroy your present.

For example, a tennis player I know would always say to herself, "You klutz, what's the matter with you?" when she missed shots. Then she would tell herself, "Straighten up!" When she would prepare for a game, she would always think in the first person: "I'm going to try to keep the ball to the right against this opponent." But when she flubbed, she would scold herself in the second person: "You dummy!" She thought about this and realized that the nagging "you" voice really was an imitation of her mother balling her out when she was a child. She'd grown up in a large family and rarely got much attention unless she did something clumsy. She was acting this out unconsciously on the tennis courts and she realized in other areas of her life as well.

Another example: I know a tennis player who told me that he would often think after a close call went against him of a building at the college he had attended years before He never knew why this seemingly unconnected image occurred to him. I suggested that he sit down and start thinking about that image and allow other thoughts and images to come into his mind, simply letting one image suggest an-other. (This technique is called "free association," and is one of many ways of gaining psychological information which can be of help to us in understanding our motives and behavior.) My friend tried this and found that his thoughts went to a college course he had taken in that building, and from there to the poor grade he felt he had unjustly been given in that course. He remembered that he had liked the instructor and that he had pleaded in vain for a reevaluation of the grade. Then he realized that he experienced the same feeling of having been done an injustice during the tennis game. As he continued to think about the situation and the feelings it aroused he realized that he often tended to play the role of the underdog who expected in advance to be thwarted. He would set himself up for disappointment, expecting it and cushioning himself unconsciously with a martyr attitude. He realized that this attitude put a barrier between him and the actualities of challenge situations. By having made it conscious, however, he was able to catch himself slipping into that attitude when it reoccurred.

Insights like these need not be rare. A lot goes on in all of our heads during a game, and if we wish we can use that material to help us understand ourselves.

The Sports Psyching techniques are useful well beyond the scope of athletics. The relaxation techniques have numerous therapeutic applications, and have been advo-cated by physicians and psychologists for daily use to help control anxieties of modern life and attendant health prob-lems. The relaxation, concentration, and Mental Rehearsal and Body Rehearsal techniques can be used in many every-day stressful situations. If you know you are going to face a job interview, a visit with the dentist, an examination, a speech, a sales presentation, or the like, you can practice for that kind of event by imagining yourself getting through it with a reasonable amount of self-assurance, focusing on the real skills required rather than on your doubts and fears.

As you have learned to take responsibility for yourself and the game on the field and to get more joy from it, you can learn to take greater responsibility for yourself in every other situation and get more satisfaction from that, too. That's playing your own game in life, and I hope that you will do it for all of the pleasure and growth it can bring.

Appendix

The Athletic Motivation Inventory

The Athletic Motivation Inventory (AMI) was designed by the Institute of Athletic Motivation in San Jose, California, a program for helping athletes attain their maximum potential and enjoyment in sports. The Institute complements coaching skills by preparing reports on athletes, based on the results of a 190-item multiple-choice questionnaire, the AMI, taken by each athlete. The reports provide coaches and athletes with valuable information on the individual athlete's attitudes related to sports. The AMI has been given to more than 75,000 athletes, including members of high school, college, and professional teams throughout the country.

The AMI is not to be confused with the Sports Emotional-Reaction Profile (Chapter 5 in this book). Whereas the SERP is designed to be used by the recreational athlete, the AMI is designed for use by athletes and coaches involved in competitive athletics at all levels. The Institute is, however, in the process of developing another Athletic Motivation Inventory specifically for the use of the recreational athlete.

A sample report prepared from the AMI is given below.

This sample is one prepared for the coach. There is another report which is similar to, and is coordinated with, the coach's report, but is shown to the individual athlete. This sample report is reprinted by permission of the institute of Athletic Motivation (ISAM), William J Winslow, President, P.O. Box 4109, San Jose, Calif. 95126.

SAMPLE ATHLETIC MOTIVATIONAL PROFILE: COACH'S REPORT

TEST TAKING ATTITUDE

Accuracy

This athlete understood the test questions and had NO DIFFICULTY in completing the AMI accurately. Therefore, this report should be highly representative of his attitudes toward athletics.

Desirability

This competitor did not attempt to present a favorable impression of himself in completing the AMI test. As a result, his trait scores were unaffected by a desire to impress others and should be reliable.

Drive: This athlete is above average in drive and ambition. He likes competition, will accept most challenges which are put to him, and prefers the odds to be even or slightly against him. Winning is important to this athlete, and competition contributes to many of his feelings of competence and personal satisfaction. He sets reasonably high goals for himself in athletics, and expects the same of his fellow athletes and the team. *Maintenance:* Set goals for this athlete that challenge his natural ability, especially if he has a high level of self confidence. Make certain that these goals are slightly higher than those he sets for himself. Directly competitive situations will have the strongest motivational effect. Immediate feedback on his performance will also be beneficial.

Aggressiveness: This athlete is above average in aggression and feels it is important in winning. He does not like to be pushed around, is free to show anger easily at anyone who betters him, and may try to get even. He releases his aggression readily and will not allow other people to take advantage of him. This is a self-assertive athlete who makes things happen and will rarely back down from an argument. *Maintenance:* Use him as a model for aggression drills because of his ability to release aggression with ease. It may be helpful to match him against equally aggressive opponents. Recognition and reward for aggressive play should have a positive effect in sustaining or possibly increasing his self-assertiveness. If he is high on leadership, he can assist others in developing their aggression.

Determination: This competitor has extremely low endurance which can negatively affect his overall performance. He resists practice sessions, considering them to be unnecessarily long and tedious, and is often out of condition. He gives up easily and cannot be counted upon to exert even an average amount of effort. During competition more determined opponents will wear him down. *Development:* It is imperative to continually work with this athlete in developing this trait. Drills which demand specific and increasing amounts of perserverance are constantly required. Strongly reward and recognize every sign of extra effort by this athlete. Reassure him that he can develop the capacity to sustain effort and try to convince him of its value in reaching his full potential in athletics.

Guilt-Proneness. This athlete is below average in guilt-proneness and is not inclined to accept personal blame when things go wrong. Even when he is responsible he may try to place the blame onto others. He does not consider physical or mental pain indispensable in realizing his potential and does not place high value on conditioning. Minor injuries can negatively affect his performance and he may use them as an excuse for poor performances. Because he is slow to admit his errors it will take longer to modify his behavior. *Development:* This athlete has to be clearly shown that he has made a mistake. This should be done as logically as possible by pointing out its exact nature. He must also understand the technical basis for the coach's suggestion, otherwise he will dismiss it as not relevant to him. Avoid accusations since it is seldom effective and encourages denial.

Leadership: This person is average in his desire to be a leader and his willingness to take charge of others. He does not seek out leadership roles but may be induced to accept them, if a stronger or more active leader is not present. He will be forceful and outspoken only on issues where he has strong personal opinions. In general, he does not perceive himself as having leadership capabilities. *Maintenance:* Possessing only a moderate inclination to lead, this athlete can dominate others only if he has other strong complimentary qualities. If you feel it is essential to place him in a leadership role, it will be necessary to support, guide and encourage his efforts. By developing a program of gradually increased leadership responsibilities, you will be able to elevate his desire for leadership.

Self Confidence: This athlete is average in his level of self confidence and has moderate faith in his athletic ability. His confidence in meeting new situations and defeating more successful opponents depends upon the circumstances and/or the particular opponent. Any strong challenge to his self assurance could cause him to experience indecisiveness and self doubt. He will not frequently speak out; however, a strong test of a value that is important to him will cause him to exert himself. *Development:* Familiarize yourself with those situations in which this athlete experiences lack of confidence and be quick to give reassurance in those cases. Reward and recognize him when he does show confidence, such as speaking out at team meetings and attaining his goals. Avoid placing him in situations where there is a high probability of failure.

Emotional Control: This individual is below average in stability and may often lose his composure. His capacity for clear thinking deteriorates under stress and his anxiety can reach a level where it has a strong negative influence on his performance. Even minor interferences will upset his concentration, and he will be slow to recover. This athlete's performances tend to be erratic and are highly influenced by unpredictable, outside forces. He also has a tendency to become overanxious before crucial contests. *Development:* It is important for this athlete that his coach recognize and anticipate those circumstances which cause him to become upset. Be quick to give reassurance when he begins to lose control, but make certain that it is done in a calm, controlled manner. Increased pressure upon him during practice will enhance his ability to retain control.

Mental Toughness: This is an extremely sensitive, tender-minded competitor who does not like to acknowledge the painful aspects of reality. This athlete is so sensitive that even minor or trivial disappointments can be upsetting. He has become accustomed to over-protection, and cannot accept personal failure without support. When subjected to criticism, his emotional reaction is so unsettling that the value of the information is greatly diminished. *Development:* Extremely gentle handling is imperative with this athlete. Harsh criticism in the presence of others will negatively affect his ability to learn. Therefore, criticism will be most beneficial when presented objectively and in private. Teach him that failure provides valuable clues for self-improvement. When he feels left out of the team, reassure him that he is part of it.

Coachability: This person is extremely receptive to coaching and accepts it as essential for personal and team development. He willingly and eagerly strives to meet all of the coach's demands and is confident that the coach's decisions are correct. In this regard, he may rely excessively upon the coach for guidance. He has high regard for the team captain and will respect his leadership as well. He is eager to learn from others and is most receptive to advice and suggestions. *Maintenance:* This competitor does not present any problems with regard to respect for coaches and the coaching process. Excessive respect, however, could lead to excessive conformity, and cause him to sacrifice his individuality. For this reason, it is recommended that you support and encourage any independent thinking and action manifested by this athlete.

Conscientiousness: This athlete's standards of right and wrong and his sense of commitment to the team are average. His willingness to accept and follow team rules will vary depending on the situation and his companions. He does not typically place his own needs above those of the team, but may occasionally prefer to do things his way. His level of conscientiousness will be enhanced or diminished depending upon his scores in "trust" and "coachability." Ambiguous or confusing team regulations will diminish his dependability. *Maintenance:* This trait can be reinforced by acknowledging his team commitment and loyalty. Show him how team requirements contribute to his personal success. When he tests or breaks rules it will be necessary to set specific limits for him. Also be aware that the coach's personal conduct can influence this athlete's attitude.

Trust: This competitor has an above average capacity to trust and readily accepts others without questioning their intentions. He places a reasonably high degree of faith in his coach and will resist becoming involved in team cliques. He effectively communicates with his fellow athletes and is not inclined to become jealous of them. This athlete also possesses high tolerance for outside threats and will not be seriously threatened by them. *Maintenance:* This favorable trait can be maintained or elevated by the examples you set for trustworthiness. By nurturing this attitude you can enhance both his capacity to learn and his personal commitment to sport and the team. Because trust is a fundamental element of team morale and cohesiveness, it would be mutually advantageous to maximize its influence in this athlete's personality.

Conclusion: The information contained in this report is based on extensive research with thousands of athletes. In preparing the report, this individual was compared with other athletes in the same sport and level of competition. We recommend that each report be reviewed with the athlete, in a private meeting, and he be granted the opportunity to comment on the results. Although these traits are important contributors to athletic success, other aspects of the athlete's life must also be taken into consideration in the coaching process. Finally, please remember that the AMI test and this Athletic Motivational Report were designed specifically for athletics, and therefore may not be applicable to other areas of the athlete's life.

Bibliography

Alderman, R.B., *Psychological Behavior in Sports.* Philadelphia: W.B. Saunders Company, 1974.

Benson, Herbert, *The Relaxation Response.* New York: William Morrow & Co., 1975.

Berne, Eric, *What Do You Say After You Say Hello?* New York: Grove Press, 1972.

Biesser, Arnold, *The Madness in Sports: Psychosocial Observations.* New York: Appleton-Century-Crofts, 1967.

Bloomfield, Harold H., Michael Peter Cain, Dennis T. Jaffe, and Robert B. Kory, *Transcendental Meditation: Discovering Inner Energy and Overcoming Stress.* New York: Delacorte Press, 1975.

Bouton, Jim, *Ball Four: My Life and Hard Times Throwing Knuckle Ball in the Big Leagues,* edited by Leonard Shecter. New York: World Publishing Company, 1970.

——— *I'm Glad You Didn't Take It Personally,* edited by Leonard Shecter. New York: William Morrow & Co., 1971.

——— with Neil Offen, *I Managed Good but Boy Did They Play Bad.* Chicago: Playboy Press, 1972.

Carr, Rachel E., *The Yoga Way to Release Tension.* New York: Coward, McCann & Geoghegan, 1974.

Coleman, John E., *The Quiet Mind*. New York: Harper & Row, Publishers, 1971.

Cratty, Bryant J., *Psychology in Contemporary Sport: Guidelines for Coaches and Athletes*. Englewood Cliffs, N.J.: Prentice-Hall, 1973.

Dickey, Glenn, *The Jock Empire: Its Rise and Deserved Fall*. Radnor, Pa.: Chilton Book Company, 1974.

Fink, David Harold, *Release from Nervous Tension*. New York: Simon & Schuster, 1962.

Fisher, Craig, editor, *The Psychology of Sport*. Palo Alto, Calif.: Mayfield Publishing Company, 1976.

Gallwey, W. Timothy, *The Inner Game of Tennis*. New York: Random House, 1974.

Geba, Bruno Hans, *Breathe Away Your Tension*. New York: Random House, 1973.

Herrigel, Eugen, *Zen in the Art of Archery*, translated by R.F.C. Hull. New York: Pantheon Books, 1953.

Hinrichsen, Gerda, *The Body Shop: Scandanavian Exercises for Relaxation*. New York: Taplinger Publishing Co., 1974.

Hoch, Paul, *Rip-Off: The Big Game—the Exploitation of Sports by the Power Elite*. Garden City, N.Y.: Anchor Books, 1972.

Humphreys, Christmas, *Concentration and Meditation: A Manual of Mind Development*, 3rd ed. Berkeley, Calif.: Shambala Publications, 1969.

Jacobson, Edmund, *Anxiety and Tension: A Physiologic Approach*. Philadelphia: J.B. Lippincott Company, 1964.

——— *Biology of Emotions*. Springfield, Ill.: Charles C Thomas, Publisher, 1967.

——— *Progressive Relaxation: A Physiological and Clinical Investigation of Muscular States and Their Significance in Psychological and Medical Practice*, 2nd ed. Chicago: University of Chicago Press, 1938.

——— *You Must Relax! A Practical Method of Reducing the*

Strains of Modern Living, 4th ed. New York: McGraw-Hill Book Company, 1957.

Jenkins, Dan, *The Dogged Victims of Inexorable Fate.* Boston: Little, Brown and Company, 1970.

Kane, J.E., *Psychological Aspects of Physical Education and Sport.* London: Rutledge Kegan-Paul, 1972.

Kenyon, Gerald S., editor, *International Congress of Sports Psychology: A Symposium, Washington, D.C., 1968.* Rome: International Institute of Sports Psychology, 1970.

Lamott, Kenneth Church, *Escape from Stress: How to Stop Killing Yourself.* New York: G.P. Putnam's Sons, 1974.

Laver, Rod, with Bud Collins, *The Education of a Tennis Player.* New York: Simon & Schuster, 1971.

Lawther, John D., *Sport Psychology.* Englewood Cliffs, N.J.: Prentice-Hall, 1972.

Leonard, George, *The Ultimate Athlete: Re-visioning Sports, Physical Education and the Body.* New York: The Viking Press, 1975.

McIntosh, Peter C., *Sports in Society.* London: C.A. Walter, 1963.

Meggyesy, Dave, *Out of Their League,* Berkeley, Calif.: Ramparts Press, 1970.

Murphy, Mike, *Golf in the Kingdom.* New York: The Viking Press, 1972.

Nicklaus, Jack, with Ken Bowden. *Golf My Way.* New York: Simon & Schuster, 1974.

Oglvie, Bruce C., and Thomas A. Tutko, *Problem Athletes and How to Handle Them.* London: Pelham Press, 1966.

Plimpton, George, *The Bogey Man.* New York: Harper & Row, Publishers, 1968.

——— *One for the Record: The Inside Story of Hank Aaron's Chase for the Home-run Record.* New York: Harper & Row, Publishers, 1974.

——— *Out of My League.* New York: Harper & Row, Publishers, 1961.

——— *Paper Lion.* New York: Harper & Row, Publishers, 1966.

Roon, Karin, *Karin Roon's New Way to Relax,* 2nd ed. New York: Greystone Corporation, 1961.

Rathbone, Josephine Langworth, *Teach Yourself to Relax.* Englewood Cliffs, N.J.: Prentice-Hall, 1957.

Sample, Johnny, *Confessions of a Dirty Ball Player.* New York: Dial Press, 1970.

Scott, Jack, *The Athletic Revolution.* New York: The Free Press, 1971.

Shaw, Gary, *Meat on the Hoof.* New York: St. Martin's Press, 1972.

Simon, Ruth Bluestone, *Relax and Stretch.* New York: Walker & Company, 1973.

Singer, Robert, *Coaching Athletes and Psychology.* New York: McGraw-Hill Book Company, 1972.

Slusher, Howard S., *Man, Sport and Existence: A Critical Analysis.* Philadelphia: Lea & Febiger, 1967.

Smith, Adam, *Powers of Mind.* New York: Random House, 1975.

Stough, Carl, with Reece Stough, *Dr. Breath: The Story of Breathing Coordination.* New York: William Morrow & Co., 1972.

Thomas, Vaughn, *Science and Sport: How to Measure and Improve Athletic Performance.* Boston: Little, Brown and Company, 1970.

Tutko, Thomas A., and Patsy Neal, *Coaching Girls and Women: Psychological Perspectives.* Boston: Allyn and Bacon, 1972.

——— and Jack Richards, *Coach's Practical Guide to Athletic Motivation.* Boston: Allyn and Bacon, 1972.

——— and Jack Richards, *The Psychology of Coaching.* Boston: Allyn and Bacon, 1971.

Vander-Zwaag, Harold J., *Toward a Philosophy of Sport.* Reading, Mass.: Addison-Wesley Publishing Co., 1972.

Weiss, Paul, *Sport: A Philosophic Inquiry.* Carbondale, Ill.: Southern Illinois University Press, 1969.

Dr. Thomas Tutko has been a consultant to many professional and college teams, among them the Pittsburgh Steelers, Dallas Cowboys, Golden State Warriors, Oakland A's, the University of Nebraska, and the University of Southern California. He is the author or coauthor of four leading texts on coaching.

Umberto Tosi is a freelance writer and coauthor of *High Treason*.